Thomas Edward Gordon

The roof of the world

A narrative of a journey over the high plateau of Tibet to the Russian frontier and

the Oxus sources on Pamir

Thomas Edward Gordon

The roof of the world
A narrative of a journey over the high plateau of Tibet to the Russian frontier and the Oxus sources on Pamir

ISBN/EAN: 9783742835376

Manufactured in Europe, USA, Canada, Australia, Japa

Cover: Foto ©Andreas Hilbeck / pixelio.de

Manufactured and distributed by brebook publishing software (www.brebook.com)

Thomas Edward Gordon

The roof of the world

THE
ROOF OF THE WORLD

BEING

THE NARRATIVE OF A
JOURNEY OVER THE HIGH PLATEAU OF TIBET
TO THE RUSSIAN FRONTIER AND THE
OXUS SOURCES ON PAMIR

BY

Lieutenant-Colonel T. E. GORDON, C.S.I.

HONORARY AIDE-DE-CAMP TO THE VICEROY OF INDIA
LATELY ATTACHED TO THE SPECIAL MISSION TO KASHGHAR

ILLUSTRATED WITH SIXTY-SIX DRAWINGS DONE ON THE SPOT
AND MAP

EDINBURGH
EDMONSTON AND DOUGLAS
MDCCCLXXVI

[*All Rights reserved.*]

PREFACE.

I HAVE avoided in this narrative going into detail concerning those countries which have already been fully described by modern European travellers, and accordingly little is said about the well-known route from Leh to Yarkand, and thence to Kashghar. I offer my sketches so far, more to illustrate the works and writings of Thompson, Shaw, Hayward, Henderson, and Bellew, than my short account of it and its scenes. Where we left the old trodden paths, as in the Tian Shan and Pamir highlands, I have attempted a more minute account of what we saw and heard in those new fields of exploration and research.

My book, however, makes no pretension to be in any way a record of scientific exploration: it merely relates what fell under "every-day" observation, with the addition of occasional information gathered here and there as we travelled. The idea of my writing it was suggested by my sketches forming such a complete series "from the Indus to the Oxus" as to merit publication simply on the ground of representing to a very great extent life and scenery *never before pictured*. In considering the form of descriptive text to accompany the sketches, I decided on that of a narrative as better calculated to give interest to the work.

The whole of the Illustrations (with the exception of the four coloured plates) are facsimile copies of my sketches made on the spot, being reproductions under the litho-photographic process, executed by Messrs. GEORGE WATERSTON and SON of Hanover Street, Edinburgh. I trust that the authenticity of these sketches, made from nature in localities most of which are entirely new to us in illustration, will compensate in some degree for occasional roughness and want of pictorial effect. The four coloured plates are faithful copies of my original water-colour drawings.

I desire to thank my travelling companions, Captains Biddulph and Trotter, for kind assistance in the subject matter of this book. Captain Biddulph, besides furnishing that which I have acknowledged in the text, helped me in the account of the form of Budhism now obtaining in Tibet, to which Captain Molloy, British Joint Commissioner at Leh, also obligingly contributed. The Map and all the notes of elevation above sea-level are by Captain Trotter, and in my account of our journey to Chadir Kul on the Tian Shan plateau I have borrowed from his letter published in the proceedings of the Royal Geographical Society of 15th June 1874.

Fergan, the latest Russian territorial acquisition in Central Asia, extends the frontier of that Power down towards the scene of our Pamir exploration; and, influenced as the adjoining small States must necessarily be by their strong neighbour, the opportunity will doubtlessly soon be given for a complete examination of the interesting regions near the head waters of the Oxus which remain yet unexplored.   T. E. GORDON.

2 ROYAL PARADE,
CHELTENHAM, 1st May 1876.

CONTENTS.

CHAPTER I.

Arrival at Leh, on the Indus—Preparations for the onward Journey—Hemis Monastery—Masquerade and Burlesque by the Llamas—Budhist Priesthood—Polo—Dancing Men and Women—Cordial Co-operation of Kashmir Authorities—Departure from Leh—Baggage and Riding Yaks—European Governors of Ladak—Characteristics of the Tartars—Shyok and Nubra Valleys—Pack-horses on Karakoram Journey—Dras and Kurgil Ponies—Yaks and "Zos"—Potato Cultivation in Shyok Valley . . . . . *Pages* 1-14

CHAPTER II.

Susser Pass—Shyok Stream—Winter and Summer Routes—Kumdan and Remu Glaciers—Mountain Hares—Tartar Porters—Mortality among Traders' Pack-horses—Wolves and Ravens—Karakoram Pass—Suget Pass—Karakash Valley—Yarkand Officials and Frontier—Captain Biddulph's Party joins—Chang-Chemno and Khoten Routes—Pangong Lake navigated—Load-carrying Sheep . . . 15-28

CHAPTER III.

Halt at Shahidulla—Yakub Khan, Kashghar Envoy—Special Couriers—Annual Yarkand Caravans—Party proceeds to Sanju—Kirghiz and Yaks—Sanju Pass—Bullock Carriage—Mirza Bahaudin—Abu-Bakr's Fort—Kilian Kirghiz—Mission and Envoy reach Sanju—Kargalik—Yarkand—Visit to the Governor: to the City—Dress and Appearance of the People—Streets and Bazaars—Market Day—Hunting-Eagles—Beggars—Population—Mission Quarters—Soldiers—Carts . 29-45

CHAPTER IV.

Departure for Kashghar—Post Houses—Commandant of Yangi-Hissar Fort—Guns carried by all Officials—Yangi-Hissar—Kashghar—Reception by the Atalik—City—Cotton Manufactures—Export Trade—Silk—Wool—Chinese and Tunganis—Domestic Slaves—Skating—Mechanics and Artisans . . . . . *Pages* 46-56

CHAPTER V.

Departure for the Tian Shan—Artush Valley and Stream—Russian Merchants—Toyan Valley and Stream—Forts of the Chakmak Defile—Caravan Route—Old Volcano—*Ovis Poli* and Black Ibex—Russian Kazaks and Kara Kirghiz—Herds of Ponies—Manner of Hunting *Ovis Poli*—Kirghiz Soldiers and Sportsmen—Chadir Kul Lake—Watershed—Tian Shan Range—Severe Cold—Captain Trotter's Work—Strict Church Discipline—Excavated Rooms at Artush . . 57-67

CHAPTER VI.

Captain Biddulph's Departure for Maralbashi—His Account of Journey and Country—Forest—Wild Camels—Gazelle—Hawking Pheasants and Hares—Maralbashi Town and Fort—Dolan People—Soldier's Story—Tigers—Trained Hunting-Eagles—Ancient City—Stages to Aksu—Return to Kashghar—Presents of Game—*Ovis Poli*—Black Ibex—Gazelle—Frozen Drawing Studies—Maral—Wild Boar Hunting—Mr. Forsyth's Visit to Artush—Dr. Stoliczka and Captain Trotter's Explorations—Turkish Protectorate of Kashghar—Yangi Shahr 68-88

CHAPTER VII.

The Army — Artillery — Jemadar Dadkhwah — Infantry — Taifurchis — Chinese Corps at Drill—Army System—Kashgharis—Food Supply—Transport—Annual Visit of Governors to the Capital—Khoten Revenue—Jade—China Tea Trade—Political System—Severity of the Laws—Sheep and Cattle Stealing—The Amír's Personal Government—Mission leaves Kashghar—Arrives at Yangi Hissar—Yakub, the Polish Deserter 89-102

CONTENTS. ix

CHAPTER VIII.

Departure for Sirikol—Chinese Fort—Kirghiz—Severe Winter Weather—"Strike" of Kashghari Attendants—Kirghiz Yuzbashi—Kaskasu Pass—Chihil Gumbaz—Torut Pass—Tangi Tar—Chichiklik Pass—Reach Sirikol Valley—Tashkurgan—Extent of Valley—Capture of Sirikol—Deportation and Return of Inhabitants—Origin of the People—Old Tashkurgan—Cultivation—Animals, Domestic and Wild—Climate—Source and Names of River—Taghdungbash Pamir and Kirghiz—Road to Kunjut—Slave's Story—Atalik's Fort—Tagharma and Kizil Art Plains—Great and Little Karakul Lakes—Meaning of "Sirikol" . . . . . *Pages* 103-120

CHAPTER IX.

Roof of the World—Previous Knowledge of Pamir Topography—Departure for Wakhan—Neza Tash—Rich Grass—Aktash Valley—Little Pamir: its Lake and Stream—Watershed—Sarhadd Stream—Extent of Little Pamir—Reach Sarhadd—Met by the "Mirzada"—Ibex-Hounds—Reach Kila Panja on the Oxus—Welcomed by the Mir: visit him in his Fort—Present State of Peace and Security—Tribute paid to Kabul—Population—Condition of the People—Animals—Crops—Through Trade—State Debt paid off . 121-137

CHAPTER X.

Wakhan—Friendly Relations with Kunjut—People of Kunjut—Shighnan friendly with Wakhan—My Messenger to Shighnan—Short Account of Country—Murghab (Great Karakul) River—Ruby Mines—Shiah Sect—Kafir Forts—Mir Wali supposed Murderer of Mr. Hayward—Yassin—Alif Beg of Sirikol—Slavery . . . 138-149

CHAPTER XI.

Severe Weather—Supplies—Snow on Great Pamir—Signs of Spring—Departure for Great Pamir—Captain Biddulph goes to the Little Pamir—Ali Murdan Shah's Signet Ring—Kirghiz of Great Pamir—Road—Wood's Victoria Lake—Great Pamir Watershed—Deep Snow—Pamir Paths—Captain Biddulph rejoins—Alichor and Siriz Pamirs—Rang Kul—Tashkurgan on Siriz Pamir—Wild Animals—Gigantic

CONTENTS.

Pair of *Ovis Poli* Horns—Rarefaction of the Air—Local Name of Lake Victoria—General Description of the Pamir Plateau—Meaning of "Pamir"—Hot Springs—"Bolor"—Aktash—Short Supplies—Difficult Defile—Return to Sirikol . . *Pages* 150-165

CHAPTER XII.

Return towards Yarkand—Sudden Change from Winter to Summer—Yarkand—Crops—Summer Dress of People—Leave Yarkand for Leh—Kogiar Route—Snow-Melting Floods—Yangi-Dawan Pass—Return of Winter—Karakoram Pass—Death of Dr. Stoliczka—Letter and Presents to Mir Futteh Ali Shah of Wakhan—His Death, and Succession of Ali Murdan Shah 166-172

LIST OF FULL PAGE ILLUSTRATIONS.

1. LOWER KUMDAN GLACIER, ON THE BED OF THE SHYOK STREAM (*to face page* 17) . . . . *Frontispiece.*

                                                                                               TO FACE PAGE

2. HEMIS BUDHIST MONASTERY, LADAK . . . 2
3. END OF THE UPPER KUMDAN GLACIER, ON THE SHYOK STREAM 18
4. THE REMU GLACIER, UPPER SHYOK—looking N.W.—before the snow-storm 19
5. THE REMU GLACIER, UPPER SHYOK—looking W.—Outline of the high range and peaks obscured by a snow-storm . 20
6. THE KARAKORAM PEAK, from the Southern side of the Pass of that name—Elevation of the spot from which the view taken, about 17,500 feet 22
7. VIEW FROM THE SUMMIT OF THE KARAKORAM PASS, looking N.E.; elevation 18,550 feet. A rough stone pillar erected in honour of the "Genii of the Mountain," similar to what is seen on most Himmalayan passes, shows on the left of the foreground 23
8. RIDING YAKS, mounted for the ascent of the Sanju Pass . 32
9. STREET SCENE, YARKAND 42
10. TAIFURCHIS OF THE YARKAND GOVÉRNOR'S GUARD, "FIELD PRACTICE" WITH THE TAIFU 44
11. VIEW IN THE TOYAN VALLEY, NEAR CHUNG TEREK, TIAN SHAN—looking South 60

LIST OF FULL PAGE ILLUSTRATIONS.

	TO FACE PAGE
12. PANORAMIC VIEW OF THE CHADIR KUL LAKE ON THE TIAN SHAN PLATEAU, Russian frontier; wild sheep in the foreground	65
13. THE TRAINED HUNTING GOLDEN EAGLE OF EASTERN TURKISTAN	78
14. CHINESE TAIFURCHIS, KASHGHAR ARMY	93
15. ROAD SCENE, KASHGHAR	96
16. THE YANGI SHAHR, KASHGHAR, Fort Residence of the Amir, from the roof of the Embassy Quarters—the Kizil Art Mountains in the distance, and Kirghiz Felt Tent in the court-yard of the "Elchi-Khana" in the foreground	99
17. THE MUZTAGH (TAGHARMA PEAK, 25,500 feet), from Tashkurgan, Sirikol—looking North; part of the old Fort of Varshidi on the left; and Kirghiz, Akoi, and Yaks in the foreground	119
18. THE AKTASH VALLEY—looking North-West	125
19. THE LITTLE PAMIR—looking West from near Onkul, about 20 miles east of Gazkul (the Little Pamir Lake); wild sheep in the foreground	127
20. KILA PANJA ON THE OXUS—looking East; showing the Forts and the approaches to the Great and Little Pamirs	131
21. FAMILY PARTY, INHABITANTS OF PATUR, WAKHAN	135
22. VICTORIA LAKE, GREAT PAMIR—looking West	155
23. THE AKTASH VALLEY—looking South-East—showing the Aktash rock from which the valley takes its name; ice breaking up on the Aksu in the foreground	157
24. LARGE OVIS POLI HORNS, from the Great Pamir	160
25. MAP	172

LIST OF ILLUSTRATIONS IN TEXT.

	PAGE
BAGGAGE YAK	1
MASQUERADING MONKS, LAMAS AT HEMIS . . .	5
POLO PLAY IN TIBET	8
TIBETAN BALLET-DANCERS AND VOCALISTS .	9
RIDING YAK	12
UPPER PART OF LOWER KUMDAN GLACIER	18
KARAKORAM BRANGSA	23
LOAD-CARRYING SHEEP OF TIBET . . .	27
KIRGHIZ YOUTH	31
KIRGHIZ YOUNG WOMAN	34
KIRGHIZ OLD WOMAN (GRANDMOTHER)	35
YARKANDI OFFICIAL	37
YARKANDI WOMAN, IN OUT-DOOR WINTER DRESS . .	38
YARKANDI WOMAN ” ” . .	40
A WOMAN OF SANJU	45
KHUL MUHAMMAD, COMMANDANT AT YANGI HISSAR . .	47
BAI BABA, A KHOKANDI OFFICER AT YANGI HISSAR	48
KASSIM AKHUN, ALIAS CHAWLIANG KHWAITANG .	53
USHER OF THE WHITE ROD AT YANGI HISSAR . . .	56
BLACK IBEX OF THE TIAN SHAN MOUNTAINS . . .	57
KIRGHIZ SOLDIERS AND PONIES, TIAN SHAN . .	67
THE DJERAN (GAZELLE) OF EASTERN TURKISTAN . .	71
HEAD OF THE MARAL (STAG) OF EASTERN TURKISTAN . .	85

LIST OF ILLUSTRATIONS IN TEXT.

	PAGE
Hunting Eagle seizing a Fox . . .	88
Jigit Soldier, Kashghar Army . .	90
Jigit Soldier, Kashghar Army . .	91
Kalmak Archer, Kashghar Army . . .	94
Kalmak Archer, Kashghar Army .	95
Kirghiz in Winter Dress	104
Sirikol Valley—looking South . . .	110
Kirghiz Ak-oi (White House)	120
Little Pamir Lake, Eastern End . .	121
Little Pamir Lake, Western End . . .	127
Sirikoli Attendant of Alif Beg's	137
Kafir Fort near Hissar-Wakhan . . .	138
Wakhi Falconer with Young Hawk	149
Yol Mazar (Roadside Shrine) on the Great Pamir Branch of the Oxus	150
Great Pamir (Victoria) Lake—Eastern End .	155
Double-humped Camel of Eastern Turkistan . .	165
Double-humped Camel of Eastern Turkistan . .	166
Ladies' Summer Fashions, Yarkand	168
Laden Yaks on the March	172

CHAPTER I.

ARRIVAL AT LEH, ON THE INDUS—PREPARATIONS FOR THE ONWARD JOURNEY—HEMIS MONASTERY—MASQUERADE AND BURLESQUE BY THE LAMAS—BUDHIST PRIEST-HOOD—POLO—DANCING MEN AND WOMEN—CORDIAL CO-OPERATION OF KASHMIR AUTHORITIES—DEPARTURE FROM LEH—BAGGAGE AND RIDING YAKS—EUROPEAN GOVERNORS OF LADAK—CHARACTERISTICS OF THE TARTARS—SHYOK AND NUBRA VALLEYS—PACK-HORSES ON KARAKORAM JOURNEY—DRAS AND KURGIL PONIES—YAKS AND "ZOS"—POTATO CULTIVATION IN SHYOK VALLEY.

BAGGAGE YAK.

THE return Mission from the Viceroy of India to the Amír of Kashghar, reached Leh, on the Indus, the capital of Western Tibet, on the 20th of September 1873. An advanced party, under the leadership of Captain Biddulph, had previously passed on, taking the eastern route by the Pangong Lake, and over the Lingzi Thang plains, with instructions to join the Mission head-quarters at Shahidulla, on the frontier of Yarkand.

The final arrangements for the long journey to the almost unknown land of Eastern Turkistan were made at Leh. Here the camp-followers were again inspected, and the horses, ponies, and travelling equipments finally examined as to fitness for continued severe work and exposure. The departure of the Mission had been unavoidably delayed considerably beyond the favourable time originally fixed, and provision had to be made for meeting the greater cold of the later season. Full-length sheep-skin coats, with felt stockings and coverlets, were issued to every man, to supplement the liberal supply of warm clothing previously given, and extra felt-lined blankets were also prepared for the riding and baggage-train animals. The result proved the sound economy of these careful precautions, the Mission reaching Yarkand with its establishment and baggage-train in perfect working order. Great extremes of heat and cold were felt during the journey, the thermometer in the course of three months ranging from over 100° in tents at Rawal Pindi, in the Punjab, where the camp was formed in July, to 25° below zero, as experienced by Captain Biddulph's party in October, shortly before reaching Shahidulla.

Captain Trotter and Dr. Stoliczka accompanied Captain Biddulph in advance; while Dr. Bellew, C.S.I., Captain Chapman, and myself, proceeded with the Envoy, Mr. (now Sir) Douglas Forsyth, C.B.*

Eight days were occupied at Leh in making the necessary further preparations for the journey across the Karakoram. Advantage was taken of the halt to visit the Budhist Monastery of Hemis, which enjoys a high reputation in Ladak for its wealth and sanctity. Hemis is twenty-five miles from Leh, on the south bank of the Indus. This monastery was first built in 1635 by Takchan Ralpha, a Lama, brother of the Ladak Raja Singa Namgyel, and was enlarged by Galtais Lama in 1793. During the first invasion and conquest of Ladak by Zorawur Sing in 1834-35, the monasteries escaped plunder. After the destruction of Zorawur Sing's army by the Chinese, in 1841,

* Two very able native officers, Resaidor Muhammad Afzul Khan of the 11th Bengal Cavalry, and Inspector Muhammad Ibrahim Khan of the Punjab Police, were also attached to the Mission.

THE NEW S. SERGIUS MONASTERY JAPAN

the Ladakis for a short time entertained the hope of entirely shaking off the Dogra yoke. This hope was quickly extinguished by the advance into Ladak of a fresh army under Dewan Hurrí Chund and Wuzír Lakpat Rai, on which occasion the monasteries were less fortunate. Hemis alone escaped being plundered, in consequence of the Head Lama tendering early submission to Hurrí Chund, and promising to feed the whole Dogra army for six months. The agreement was faithfully carried out; and, though the other monasteries have never recovered the losses they then experienced, Hemis has been able to retain some of its ancient glories and reputation.

The form of Budhism now obtaining in Tibet has altered somewhat since its first introduction, and differs considerably from what may be regarded as the purer form practised in Ceylon and Burma. Budhism was first introduced into Tibet in the third century B.C., by Sakya Thubba, who inculcated merely a mystical belief in the Supreme Budha. Lamaism, with its monasteries and prayer-wheels, was founded later by Urgyan Padma, a successor of Sakya Thubba, when considerable changes were made in the importance attached to forms and ceremonies, and the superior sanctity of Lamas. Later on, a reformer known as Tson Khappa appeared, who founded the sect of Gelukpa "the virtuous," and strove to bring back Budhism to its purer and simpler form. In course of time it was found that the precepts enjoined were too rigorous for frail humanity, and the sect of Kahguitpa, "believers in the succession of precepts," was founded. These now form the two sects into which Lamas are divided, but have many minor subdivisions that take their names from some celebrated monastery, retaining the distinctions of dress and tenets of the great sects from which they spring. Both sects wear a red dress, but the Gelukpas are distinguished by a yellow cap, and follow the tenets laid down in the book "Do," "the Aphorisms," which is amplified and assisted by thirty-three minor volumes. They are more puritanical in their religious observances than the Kahguitpas, and strictly abstain from meat, spirituous liquors, and marriage. The Dalai Lama of Lhassa belongs to the Gelukpa sect, which owns the Gahldang, Despung, Sera, and Tashi-Lhunpo subdivisions. The Kahguitpas wear a red cap, and practise the tenets laid down in the book Gnall or Gyuit, which is amplified in twenty minor volumes. They do not observe such strict abstinence as the Gelukpas, and, though the practice is not common, are allowed to marry. A married monk is obliged, however, to leave the monastery, and cease exercising his functions as a priest. The Lamas of Hemis belong to the sect of Kahguitpa, which owns the Dukpa, Sekya, Birgonpa, Taklung, and Sarboo subdivisions.

The resemblance between these religious subdivisions and the many monastic orders of the Roman Catholic Church is curious. It is not to be wondered at that the first Jesuit missionaries who visited Tibet, studied its system of monasteries, clerical celibacy, worship of a Trinity, and acknowledgment of a spiritual head on earth, and watched the religious services accompanied by incense-burning, music, and chanting, should have imagined that they had at last found the home of Antichrist.

Lhassa, the Rome of Budhism, is still regarded with veneration, and a great annual fair, called Shishu, is held at Hemis on the same day that similar ones are held at the Dachanchunga and Sungasooling monasteries in Lhassa, which belong to the same order.

Hemis is chiefly known to modern travellers on account of a masque performed by the monks for a small gratuity. The dresses, which are extremely grotesque, as a glance at the accompanying sketch will show, are all brought from Lhassa. The origin of the pantomime is unknown, but it is doubtless of great antiquity, possibly dating from times before the introduction of Budhism, to which it has no apparent affinity. I am not aware of any similar ceremony mentioned by travellers in countries where Budhism prevails. Through the kindness of Mr. Johnson, the Wuzír of Ladak, we were treated to a full-dress

MASQUERADING MONKS.

performance, at which the Lamas of three neighbouring monasteries assisted. The play seemed to be a pantomimic burlesque of the pomp and pleasures of a royal court. First came a band of courtiers sweeping the way for the approach of the King, then a party of musicians with children's rattles, followed by a masquerade of devils, blue, red, and white, monsters, fairies, fools and philosophers, all dancing to the loud-sounding pipe, drum, and cymbal, before the King, who came and reposed under a great canopy, looking silly and contemptuous. Our breakfast, sent on ahead, had gone astray; but the Lamas, on hearing of it, provided us with a capital repast of fowls, bread, and eggs, with tea served in coarse china.

The following account of polo played at Leh, and of the Tartar ballet, is by Captain Biddulph :—

"The game of Polo, which promises to become nationalised in England, has been played in Ladak for centuries. Every village of any pretensions has its polo (pronounced Pooloo) ground attached, consisting of a smooth space of greensward or shingle, from 200 to 300 yards long and 80 yards broad. Low parallel walls about eight or ten inches high mark the sides of the ground, the ends being left open. Cunningham, writing of Ladak more than twenty years ago, gives the following excellent description of the game :—

"'The favourite amusement of the Botis, both of Ladak and of Balti, is polo, in which all parties from the highest to the lowest can take a part. I saw the game played at Mulbil, in a field 400 yards long and 80 yards broad, which was walled round for the purpose with a stone dyke. There were twenty players on each side, all mounted on ponies and armed with sticks about four feet long, and bent at the lower end. One player took the ball and advanced alone into the middle of the field, where he threw up the ball, and as it fell, struck it towards one of the goals. The goals were formed of two upright stones placed about twenty-five or thirty feet apart. When the ball was driven through a goal, one of the successful party was obliged to dismount and pick it up; for if the opposite party should have driven it back before it was picked up, the goal did not count. The game consisted in winning a certain number of goals, either five, seven, or nine. Numerous musicians were in attendance, who made a most lively din whenever a goal was won, and the noise was increased by the cheers of the successful party.

"'The game is a very spirited one, and well calculated for the display of bold and active horsemanship. Accidental blows occur frequently, but the poor ponies are the principal sufferers. The game was once common in India under the name of Chaogan, but it is now completely forgotten. The old Chaogan-grounds still exist in every large town in the Punjab hills—in Bilaspur, Nadaon, Shujanpur, Kangra, Haripur, and Chamba, where the goal-stones are still standing. The game is repeatedly mentioned by Baber, but after his time it gradually became obsolete. It was introduced by the Mussulman conquerors, and the very first king, Kutb-ud-din Aibak, was killed by a fall from his horse when playing at Chaogan in A.D. 1210. The Pathan kings of India still continued to join in the game down to the time of Sikander Lodi in A.D. 1498, when* one day, while the king and his court were playing at Chaogan, the bat of Haibat Khan Shirwani by accident came in contact with the head of Suliman, the son of Darya Khan Lodi, who received a severe blow. This was resented on the spot by Khizir Khan, the brother of Suliman, who, galloping up to Haibat Khan, struck him violently over the skull. In a few minutes both sides joined in the quarrel, and the field was in uproar and confusion. Mahmud Khan Lodi and Khan Khanan Lodi interposing, endeavoured to pacify Haibat Khan, and succeeded in persuading him to go home quietly with them. The King, apprehensive of a conspiracy, retired immediately to the palace; but nothing more transpiring, he made another party at the same game a few days after.'

* Briggs's Ferishta.

"The main street of Leh is an old polo-ground, round which houses have been built, and many a good game is still played there. During our halt at Leh, preparing ourselves to face the Karakoram, some of our party wishing for a game, the Wuzír, Mr. Johnson, sent the requisite notice to the villages round.

"The next afternoon, at the appointed time, players, leading their shaggy little ponies, appeared from Sabu, Chushot, and other places; some having come ten or twelve miles for a game, and riding home the same evening. The street had been carefully swept and watered, and none but the players were allowed in it, except the town band, which was placed on one side half-way between the two goals. The flat roofs of the houses lining the ground were covered with lookers-on, who watched the game with unflagging interest.

POLO PLAY IN TIBET.

"Sides were chosen by all the polo sticks being thrown on the ground and divided into pairs. The two choosers of sides then took a stick from each pair; sticks were reclaimed by their owners, and the game began. Pipe and drum struck up a monotonous tune, which warmed up for a few discordant moments each time a goal was taken. The players formed a picturesque group with their streaming pig-tails, urging on

their rough little ponies with the short Tartar whip, spurs being unknown. The pace was good, and there was plenty of hard hitting. The back-handed hitting on the near side was especially good, and the length of reach greater than is usually seen among English players. From the narrowness of a Tartar polo-ground, goals are frequent, but the interest of the game does not appear to be diminished in consequence. The picking up of the ball after a goal is hit is a curious feature: if before this can be done one of the other side can hit the ball out again between the markers, which here were eighteen feet apart, the game goes on, and no goal is reckoned. After nearly two hours' play, everybody had had enough, and the proceedings terminated by a dance in the street. The performers were professional dancers, men and women. The latter were very robust

TIBETAN BALLET-DANCERS.

damsels, dressed in gay colours, with a red and green cloak hanging from their shoulders; the men were not dressed in any distinctive costume, with the exception of a flat overhanging cap and very long sleeves to their coats. The dance itself was very monotonous, the performers following one another in a circle with a slow short step and very grave faces. They would not, perhaps, have been thought remarkable for grace or beauty at Her Majesty's Theatre, but at Leh it was looked on as a wonderful display of elegance."

When travelling up the valley of the Indus, a great gathering of Tartars took place on the 12th of September to play polo before us, and the same band of dancers described by Captain Biddulph performed for our amusement at Leh. I was thus enabled to make the accompanying sketches, illustrative of both, from the life.

The most liberal arrangements were made by the Maharajah of Kashmir for the provisioning and transport of the Mission to his frontier across the Karakoram, where we were to be met by the Kashghar authorities. Food for men and animals, with a sufficient supply of firewood, was placed under a guard at every stage in the mountain wilderness beyond Changlung (the green pasture), in Nubra, the last inhabited spot on the Karakoram route. Mr. Johnson, the Governor of Ladak, carried out the Maharajah's orders in the most complete manner, so that in the icy desert of High Tartary we travelled with a degree of comfort almost equal to what we had in the Lower Himmalayas. But while the head-quarter party thus fared well, that in advance, travelling by the easterly or Chang-Chemno route, had to face difficulties and hardships, which, however, were met cheerfully and overcome successfully. They proceeded for a short distance together, and then separated to follow different tracks, and thus examine thoroughly the country to the east of the Karakoram pass. They met with greater cold, and crossed loftier heights than we did, and they experienced many discomforts to which we were strangers.

We left Leh on the 29th of September. Snow had commenced to fall on the surrounding hills, and the first day we had the thermometer at 15° by 9 P.M. We started with entirely yak transport, and kept it till the long and difficult Susser pass was left behind. The Khardung pass (17,229 feet), crossed the following day, took us to the valley of the Shyok, down which we travelled for two days, and then turned up the Nubra stream, making three marches to Changlung. Two hundred and fifty baggage ponies were here provided, to be taken into use after crossing the Susser. Heavy snow was now falling daily on the heights, and a severe journey was expected; but, fortunately for us, the snow ceased the day before we ascended from Changlung; and, so far from suffering, we benefited by what had fallen, as it filled up the spaces between the boulders and rocks, and in many places almost smoothed our path. A number of laden yaks had passed ahead and trodden down the new fall before we arrived. The yak is admirably fitted for this work, the shortness of its legs keeping it from sinking to any great depth, and instinct teaching it to avoid soft drifts where footing is difficult to find.

We used yaks for riding purposes on three occasions only: when crossing the Khardung and Sanju passes, and ascending the first rise from the Nubra valley towards the Susser. Recourse was had to yaks then, chiefly on account of the deep snow at the two first-mentioned places, and to spare our horses at the third, where the ascent is unusually long and steep. But horses can be ridden up all, as was done by many of our people. Throughout the whole of the journey to Russian Turkistan beyond Kashghar, and over the Pamir to the Oxus, I always found the paths perfectly practicable for a horse or pony.

Ladak has had the advantage, unusual in a native state, of

being for several years past under a European governor. Mr. Drew was Wuzír there for a considerable time, and on his departure, Mr. Johnson, the first successful traveller of modern times in Eastern Turkistan, was appointed to the charge. The Tartars there appreciated so thoroughly the rule of an Englishman, that when left under a native governor for a short time after Mr. Drew's departure, a number of them are said to have gone to Srinuggur to complain in person to the Maharajah. The Tartars throughout Ladak are under "Kardars" (Headmen) of their own class, whom the Maharajah appoints. Foreigners (Hindus and others) were tried in this capacity, but the people would not accept them. They are said to suffer to any extent under a Tartar Kardar without complaining, but in no way can be made contented under a stranger so placed over them. The explanation probably is that they are as a rule well treated by the one, and not by the other. They are peaceful, patient, and hardy; and if to their quality of extraordinary power of endurance were added that of courage, they would be invaluable as soldiers in those regions. But the Tartars of Ladak are more inclined to arms than their neighbours, and the Maharajah of Kashmir has made a beginning towards utilising them in a military capacity. There is now a Ladaki corps, numbering over 100 men, stationed at Leh, and employed in the surround-

RIDING YAK.

ing district. The men are obtained by conscription, and are tolerably well paid. They are said to take quickly to the use of arms, and to give promise of being faithful and brave under a leader whom they believe in. This corps furnished the men who protected the supplies laid out for our Mission on the uninhabited part of the Karakoram road between Leh and the Yarkand frontier.

The Shyok and Nubra valleys show signs of increasing prosperity, the result, I believe, of the fostering care bestowed upon Ladak by Messrs. Drew and Johnson, at the instance of His Highness Rumbhir Sing, the present Maharajah of Kashmir, whose state expenditure in that province considerably exceeds the income. The inhabitants of these valleys benefit considerably by the Yarkand trade, in selling flour, grain, and forage for the "kafilas" of pack horses passing and repassing. All the jungle and grass lands near the villages are carefully enclosed with strong thorn fences for grazing purposes, a charge being made for the horses when turned in. Lucerne grass is extensively grown, and similarly enclosed for grazing. The traders feed their horses well before entering upon the severe portion of the Karakoram journey, which extends for eleven stages from the Nubra valley to the Karakash river near Shahidulla, over a wild, desolate, and elevated country destitute of grass. While passing over this distance, a few pounds of barley only form the daily food of the trader's pack horse, which generally carries a load of 240 lbs., inclusive of the saddle. Grass is neither good nor plentiful at Shahidulla, and forage, such as a horse requires after the Karakoram journey, is not obtainable till Sanju, six stages farther on, with the difficult pass of that name intervening, is reached. Accordingly the fodder and supplies of the Nubra and Shyok valleys are in great demand in the "kafila" coming and going seasons, to prepare for and recover from the effects of this killing work. The stages there are very short, and the traders move leisurely along, halting and marching according to the condition of their horses. The 250 ponies which I have mentioned as joining our camp to relieve the baggage yaks, were sent on to these pastures to pick up their last grass before commencing the toilsome journey beyond. These ponies were strong hardy animals from Dras and Kurgil, districts lying between Ladak and Kashmir. Ponies are extensively bred at these places, and the Kashmir state can always depend upon obtaining a great number there, when transport on a large scale is wanted. Ladak can similarly furnish very many yaks, but they are of no use lower than Leh, being only capable of work at high altitudes. The yak is a slow beast of burden, becoming footsore if driven fast or far. It is invaluable when time is no object, carrying as it does a very heavy load, and finding its own food in the most unlikely and impossible looking places. The "zo," which appears to be the link between the cow and the yak, is found below Leh, and is much used for carriage purposes. In connection with the Shyok and Nubra valleys it may be interesting to know that Mr. Johnson has introduced the potato there, and with success, as proved by an excellent crop grown in 1873 at the village of Deskit, near the junction of the Shyok and Nubra streams. It is considered probable that the Tartars will now carry on the cultivation.

CHAPTER II.

SUSSER PASS—SHYOK STREAM—WINTER AND SUMMER ROUTES—KUMDAN AND REMU GLACIERS—MOUNTAIN HARES—TARTAR PORTERS—MORTALITY AMONG TRADERS' PACK-HORSES—WOLVES AND RAVENS—KARAKORAM PASS—SUGET PASS—KARAKASH VALLEY—YARKAND OFFICIALS AND FRONTIER—CAPTAIN BIDDULPH'S PARTY JOINS—CHANG-CHEMNO, AND KHOTEN ROUTES—PANGONG LAKE NAVIGATED—LOAD-CARRYING SHEEP.

THE cold steadily increased as we progressed. We left the Nubra valley on the 6th of October, and encamped that night at the foot of the Susser pass, the most difficult in the whole journey. The thermometer marked 11°. The pass was crossed the following day without any mishap, notwithstanding the great extent of snow and ice, which, especially at the last part of the ascent, caused much scrambling and struggling among men and horses. The state of the numerous huge glaciers clinging to the sides of the overhanging mountains, and presenting the appearance of being merely temporarily checked in their downward course, points to the probability of this pass being choked up at no very distant date, and obstructed for traffic, similarly as that which leads from near the head of the Kufelung source of the Yarkand river into the Nubra valley is said to have been. This latter was in ancient times on the main route by which the hosts of mounted invaders crossed into Little Tibet, but now it is only passable by men on foot. At present, the only travellers by it, are the hardy inhabitants of

Baltistan, to whom it makes a great saving of time and distance when communicating with their brethren who have settled in Yarkand. A colony of Baltis has long existed at Yarkand, chiefly engaged in agriculture, and a journey to and fro is made every year. The thermometer marked 18° at 3 P.M. on the summit of the Susser pass (17,800 feet), and it sank during the night to 6° below zero.

On descending the pass we again came upon the Shyok, which we had crossed and left a few days before. The Shyok is the principal mountain tributary of the Indus, and rises in the Karakoram mountains to the south-east of that pass. It flows south-east to as far south as Leh, when it turns abruptly to the north-west, and continues in that direction till the Indus is reached at Keris. Its upper course is rushing and turbulent down a narrow glen, but its middle course is either broad or rapid, or divided into numerous branches; in the lower part it is generally a furious rapid, confined between precipitous cliffs. In the depth of winter, when completely frozen, the stream is followed for a great part of the Karakoram journey, thus avoiding the troublesome Sussér pass, and the long road over the high Dipsang plain, both of which come in the summer route. The precipitous nature of its banks and the adjoining mountains prevent any passage along it when the ice breaks up. Mr. Johnson arranged to return by the river route on his way back after parting with us at the frontier, to examine the locality, with the view of bringing engineering skill to bear on its difficulties; but I believe that the necessary operations to open a road were found to be too extensive to be undertaken at present. Considering the extraordinary and extreme difficulties of climate and want of grass always to be met with in this direction, it would, I think, be far more profitable for our commerce to seek out a new trade route to Eastern Turkistan by which the severe and barren elevated wastes of the Karakoram may be avoided.

Winter having set in severely when we reached the Shyok again on the 9th of October, the partially frozen and low state of the stream admitted of our passing up it towards its source. The supplies, however, having been laid out on the summer route over the Dipsang plain, in anticipation of our earlier journey as expected, the main portion of the camp was sent that way, while we proceeded by the winter path. We took a few yaks to carry the supplies, and the rest were sent back, the ponies furnished in Nubra being taken into use. We passed the lower Kumdan glacier the first day. It comes from the high peaks to the north-west, and continues down the right bank of the stream for over two miles, forming a perfect wall of ice rising from the water about 120 feet, and showing a surface covered with countless pinnacles and points. Portions of it yet stand at several places on the opposite bank, where the original mass was forced against the great up-rising red cliffs, and blocked up the stream, thus forming a lake, which at last burst this ice barrier by the increasing pressure of its collected waters.

We encamped that night at Kumdan under a high cliff on the deep shingly bed of the old lake formed in the manner just described. I remained behind the party sketching the various remarkable parts of the glacier, and often in making my way through the stream got into the line of baggage yaks, which, moving in their usual leisurely manner, appeared to me to run the chance of being caught in the forming ice. The cold was excessive, as shown by the mass of icicles on the long-haired yaks and rough-coated ponies when

UPPER PART OF LOWER KUMDAN GLACIER.

they emerged from the stream. The doubtful nature of the narrow fords, and the painful prospect of a possible accidental dip in the stream in such a low state of temperature, checked all attempt to hasten forward by leaving the line of cautious deliberative yaks. The great peaks from which the lower Kumdan glacier springs, had their "snow banners" in full display as we passed up, these being the continuous light clouds of powdery snow blown off the surface, similar to what is seen in the Alps.

On the 10th we continued in the same general northerly direction, and passed the upper Kumdan glacier, which shoots down from a lateral valley to the north-west, and almost touches the opposite side of the main valley. It probably, at one time, formed the barrier for a long and extensive shallow lake above. We encamped that night at Gipshun, in a ravine close to the broad pebbly bed of the Shyok. A little scattered

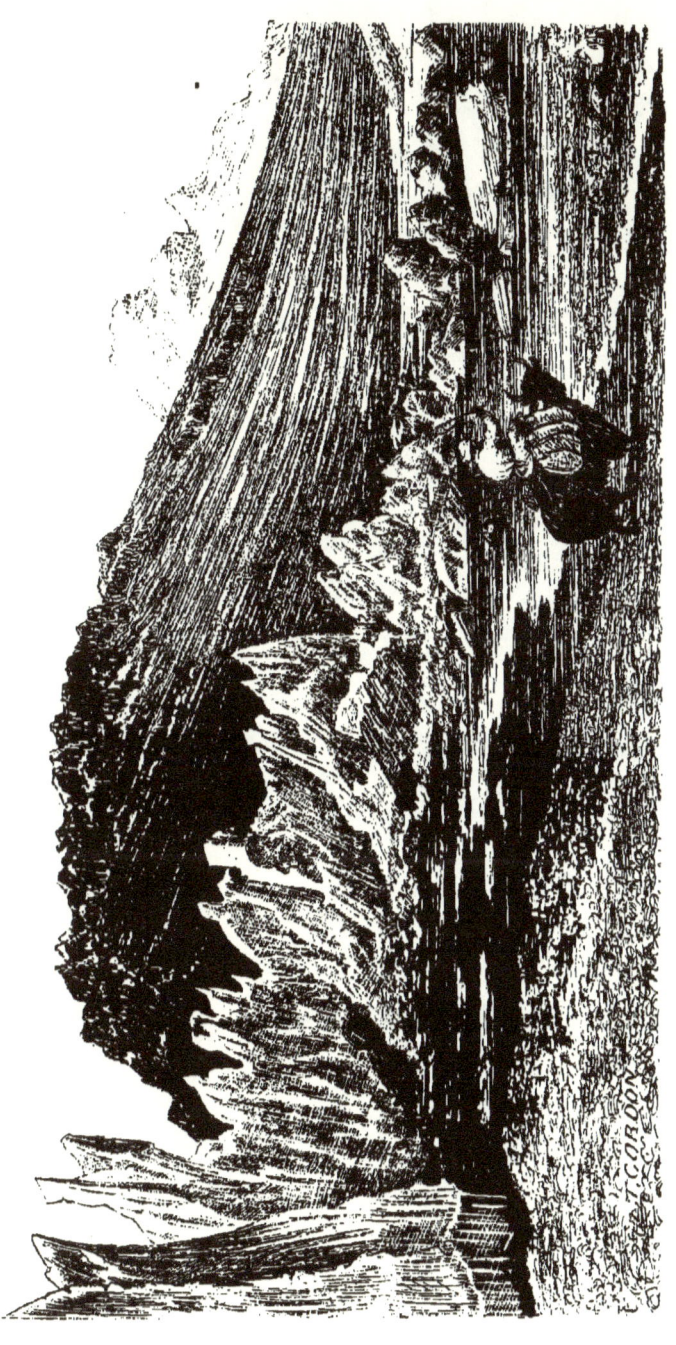

END OF THE UPPER KUMDAN GLACIER – SHYOK VALLEY

REMU GLACIER UPPER SHYOK – LOOKING N.W

and scanty grass appears in the soft hollows about here, making the neighbourhood, as we were told, an occasional haunt of the huge wild yak, and the graceful Tibetan antelope. I went up towards the great Remu glacier to the north-west, in quest of wild yaks, the fresh marks of which I had noticed; but I saw no game except a couple of mountain hares, which are found in small numbers all over this wild country. On the return journey the following year, the two ibex-hounds we brought from Wakhan coursed them to no purpose, on the Karakoram, at an elevation of over 17,000 feet. There the hares had by far the advantage of the dogs, which soon came to a stand-still, panting and breathless from the extreme rarefaction of the air. The hares, on the contrary, held on their way without any apparent inconvenience. I found the Remu glacier too distant to allow of reaching and returning before nightfall, so I had to make my way back to camp, from a point about two miles short of it. The thermometer marked 2° below zero that night, and the danger of being benighted in such a climate was too great a risk to run.

The following day we passed up the Daolat-Beg-uldi stream bed to the east of north, and as we crossed the great gravelly flat at its junction with the Shyok, we had a very fine view of the north-western portion of the Remu glacier, which showed right down in the main valley, with an even surface, wonderfully sea-like. After proceeding farther, and looking back, a truly magnificent sight appeared—a great glacier from the valley to the west, joined by several from its lateral ravines, and uniting in the plain below with that from the north-west to form one extended sea of ice. Above them rose stupendous peaks, whose outline was lost in the snow-storm clouds which hung about them. As far as the personal observation of European travellers has noted, this great Remu glacier stands unrivalled in its grandeur of extent and close resemblance to a frozen sea.

The glaciers of the Western Himmalayas are twice as extensive as those of the Alps, and are probably the largest in the world, or, at all events, larger than any others out of the Polar regions. One in the Muztagh range is believed to be 34 miles long, with fifteen distinct moraines; while in its immediate vicinity is another 31 miles in length, which may be said to join with it in making 65 miles of continuous ice. The Remu glacier, shown in the accompanying sketches, rises amongst peaks and ridges from 19,000 to 24,000 feet high. It is about 21 miles in length, and from 1 to $1\frac{3}{4}$ mile broad, terminating at an elevation of 15,800 feet above the sea with a width of about 3 miles of gigantic cliffs of ice fully 250 feet high. This glacier, owing to the action of the river Shyok, comes to an end at a much greater altitude than glaciers in that part of the Himmalayan system generally do. The river, cutting away successive blocks of ice, usually prevents farther extension. The glacier, however, has been known on several occasions to protrude right across the valley of the Shyok, so as to dam up the stream and form a large lake, ending in a cataclysm when the water finally bursts through the ice and rushes down the valley in a mighty and destructive flood wave, similarly as has been observed of the Kumdan glaciers lower down.

The whole country around is singularly desolate-looking. It was believed for some time that the disastrous inundation of the Indus in 1841 was caused by the damming up of the Shyok by these glaciers; but the later opinion of some well acquainted with Ladak, who went closely into the question,

THE REMU GLACIER – UPPER-SHYOK, LOOKING W

inclines to the belief that that mighty flood-wave resulted from a huge landslip blocking up the main river somewhere in the unknown portion of its course lying in Dilail and Chilas, near the Punjab frontier, where it is said to be unusually confined and shut in by precipitous cliffs and high steep mountains. We met our camp again at Daolat-Beg-uldi, which place it reached in three stages of 43 miles in all, from the Shyok, while the route we followed made the distance about 30 miles, a great saving in such an inhospitable waste.

The elevation of Daolat-Beg-uldi is 16,700 feet. It lies on the verge of the Dipsang plateau, about 17,500 feet high, which we crossed on our return journey. The distress in man and beast produced by rarefaction of the air, which had troubled us on the Khardung pass, lasted for a very short time, as the descent there led down to comparatively low ground, but the Susser landed us on the high undulating bleak plateau which extends for about 100 miles from that pass on the south to the Suget on the north, and our party suffered continuously more or less during the seven days occupied in marching over it.

An energetic Hindu trader arrived at Daolat-Beg-uldi the same day as ourselves, pushing on with his goods for the Yarkand market. The anxiety of the Maharajah of Kashmir to provide against all possible mishap was such that double the amount of supplies required for our camp was laid out over the Karakoram, and accordingly the local carriage, generally available for traders, was fully engaged in this service. The great demand for transport having raised the charges to one rupee (about two shillings) per load of 80 lbs. per stage, the Ladaki porters undertook the carriage of goods at these remunerative rates, and Kan Chand, the trader I have referred to, was on his way over with eighty porters, each carrying a load of nearly 80 lbs. weight. The fact that these men, so laden, made an average daily journey of fourteen miles for eleven days, over the high desert regions of Tibet, under peculiarly distressing conditions of climate, proves the great endurance of the Ladakis previously noticed.

The skeletons of horses lie in numbers round the halting-places and along the mountain desert road. The extreme dryness of the air in this rainless region, and the intense cold, kill all putrid tendencies, and there is no smell of decaying matter. Ravens appeared to follow our camp the whole way over, on the outlook for the usual casualties among the pack animals. Wolves are also said to frequent the route with the same object, but I did not hear or see any during the journey. Both ravens and wolves were disappointed of their usual feast when following our "kafila," as the excellence and liberality of the transport arrangements prevented any horses or ponies being worked to death, though, as might be expected with such a large number, a few died from other causes.

We crossed the Karakoram pass (18,550 feet) on the 12th of October. Starting from our high camp at Daolat-Beg-uldi, and halting that night at Karakoram Brangsa on the other side, at an elevation of 17,030 feet, we found the ascent and descent comparatively easy, but the "head troubles" from the great altitude increased in many of the party to a disagreeable extent. I hesitated long on the summit of the pass before I could make up my mind to sit down and sketch. While I was at work with my pencil, two wagtails hopped about me, quite at home apparently there, 18,550 feet above the sea.

The whole of the country in this high-lying mountain desert

THE KARAKORAM PEAK - FROM THE SOUTHERN SIDE OF THE PASS - LOOKING N. W.

VIEW FROM THE SUMMIT OF THE KOKIHINUI PASS, 4515 FT. 1084 M.

is singularly wild and desolate looking. There is nothing strikingly grand in the scenery, excepting the glaciers: the mountains, rising as they do from such an elevated level, appear mere hills. This was particularly noticeable in the view from the top of the pass. There is a great absence of rock and precipice, and gravel spreads far and wide over the slopes and flats. The capped peak shown in the sketch of the southern side of the pass is called Karakoram (black gravel), from the dark gravel which crumbles from the rock at its summit. This is the peak which gives its name to the range.

KARAKORAM BRANGSA.

Snow commenced to fall in the evening, at our camp at Karakoram Brangsa, and continued throughout the night, and the following morning found the whole country deeply covered with it. We made a long march of 26 miles to Aktagh, to escape from it, and after one day's halt there crossed the Suget pass (17,618 feet), and reached the Karakash valley in a day's journey of 28 miles. We were glad to escape from the heights, where the cold at our last camp reached to 15° below zero. Captain Trotter and Dr. Stoliczka joined us from the eastern route the day after we crossed the Karakoram. We came upon grass and wood at Suget, four miles from Shahidulla, and halted there a day, to give our tired cattle a rest. We were there met by some of the Yarkand officials, who came from Shahidulla to receive and entertain us with the usual profuse hospitality of the country, in the form of a "dastar-khwan" (table-cloth) of soups, stews, sweets, bread, fruit, and tea. The place, with its bushes, grass, and running water, appeared charming to us after the barren frozen wastes of the Karakoram. The air, notwithstanding 7° of frost at night, felt soft and mild in comparison to what we had just left.

We moved to Shahidulla on the 17th. Here we were received by the Yarkand authorities, those of Kashmir having accompanied us, and arranged for our progress so far. The former had a number of Kirghiz yaks ready to relieve our baggage ponies. Very tired did the ponies look after their hard march and heavy work in the rarefied air of the Karakoram heights. Mr. Johnson gave a feast of many sheep to the Ladak, Kurgil, and Dras men, previous to the return journey with him to Nubra and Leh.

Captain Biddulph joined on the 18th, and then, for the first time, the whole of the officers of the mission were assembled together in camp. Captain Biddulph's party brought very complete reports of the Chang-Chemno route. Notwithstanding the easier nature of the country there, and the belief which at one time prevailed, that the traders were anxious to adopt it in preference to the Karakoram road, the latter continues to be used by them to the total exclusion of the former. The old road offers to them the advantages of a considerable saving in distance on the whole journey, and less ground to pass over, where carriage of food for man and beast is absolutely necessary,—advantages which, in their experience, outbalance the toil and risks of a rougher route and the severe Susser pass.

Khoten is the most flourishing, and in point of productive industry the most important of the provinces of Kashghar. It has no direct trade with India, though it is very advantageously situated for such. The desire is to keep Khoten secluded on account of its gold fields, which contribute largely to the state treasury. An easy route from Leh leads over the less elevated plains to the east of the Lingzi Thang, by the Pangong lake and the vicinity of Rudok, to Polu, the frontier village of Khoten in that direction. The great superiority of this route consists in fuel being abundant, and a good supply of grass procurable throughout; it is, moreover, said to be quite practicable for the hardy Bactrian camel, which is extensively bred and used in Khoten. But a great portion of it lies in Chinese territory; and while the "pushm" (shawl wool) merchants of the adjoining districts under British and Kashmir rule are permitted to frequent the Rudok district markets, the national obstructive policy is opposed to any through traffic.

Captain Trotter carried on his journey an indiarubber boat, by means of which he and Captain Biddulph navigated for the first time the waters of the Pangong lake, lying at the great elevation of 13,900 feet above the sea. The party was accompanied by a flock of the load-carrying sheep of Tibet, laden with flour and grain, a description of which is given in Moorcroft's *Travels* and Cunningham's *Ladak*. The following is Captain Biddulph's account of this novel transport train with which he joined our camp at Shahidulla :—

"I left Tankse on 18th September, taking with me thirty sheep carrying loads of grain and flour. Wishing merely to test their marching capabilities, I looked upon the supplies they carried as extra, and their loads remained intact till within four marches of Shahidoolla, when I was forced to commence using them.

"The Tartars usually make their sheep carry a load of 32 lbs., and march seven or eight miles a day only, making frequent halts; as, however, I expected to be marching hard at times, I put only a load of 20 lbs. on each sheep. Beyond this I took no care of them, and they simply took their chance.

"A great part of the route was over rough and stony ground, but only one sheep broke down, though many of them showed signs of footsoreness at times.

"The loads, secured by breast and breech ropes, ride well, sinking into the fleece, and not being liable to shift.

"On fair ground, where they travelled with a broad front, they marched at the rate of one and three-quarter mile an hour; a large number would no doubt travel slower, and much must depend on the breadth of the road.

"The greatest difficulty they had to contend with was crossing streams, and while marching in the Karakash valley they were sometimes obliged to cross the river three or four times in a day. Not only were their loads liable to become damaged, but the weight of water hanging in their fleeces, and on several occasions freezing, greatly impeded progress.

"On the days on which they had no grass, they had literally nothing to eat, as they refused grain, not being accustomed to it.

"One man was sufficient to manage the lot, and two men, I should say, could easily drive and manage a hundred.

"On arrival in camp they were unloaded, and turned out to shift for themselves till dark, when they were herded for the night.

"The fact that a flock of sheep carrying 20 lbs. loads should be able to march 330 miles in a month with only one casualty, through a country in which forage is always scanty, and at a very inclement season of the year, is remarkable. After the first march the elevation was never less than 11,000 feet, and the thermometer at night sank to 15° and 16° below zero. The sheep, however, apparently did not feel either cold or elevation. Future exploring parties on the Karakoram will, I feel certain, find a flock of sheep a most useful addition to their camp. Not only are they very easily looked after, but they can feed themselves as they go along, which ponies cannot do, and can pick up a subsistence on the scanty pasture grounds and among the rocks where horses would starve. Besides this, when their loads are disposed of, they can themselves be eaten.

LOAD-CARRYING SHEEP OF TIBET.

"The accompanying Table will show the particulars of the marches they made. I was accompanied the whole time by a Survey Pundit, who paced the distance each day.

"TABLE SHOWING MARCHES TAKEN BY A FLOCK OF THIRTY SHEEP CARRYING LOADS OF 20 LBS.

March.	Date.	Miles.	Remarks.
	1873.		
Tankse to Tchur-ka-talab	18th Sept.	14	
Lukung	19th ,,	7¼	
Chagra	21st ,,	8	
Rimdi	22d ,,	13	Cross Lunkar La, 18,400 feet.
Pamzal	23d ,,	13	
Gogra	24th ,,	12½	
Shummal Lungpa	26th ,,	12	
Camp near Nischn	27th Sept.	14¼	No grass. Cross Changlung La, 19,300 feet.
,, on Lingzi Thung	28th ,,	16½	No grass.
Camp	29th ,,	20¼	No grass.
Sumnal	30th ,,	21½	Cross Kizzil Dawan, 17,600 feet; did not arrive in camp till dark.
Kizzil Jilga	1st Oct.	11	
Chung Tash	7th ,,	24	Grass very scarce; did not arrive till after dark.
Sumnal	9th ,,	13	
Camp	10th ,,	10¼	Grass very scarce.
,,	11th ,,	15	No grass.
,,	12th ,,	16¾	No grass. One sheep broke down on march.
Sorah	13th ,,	5½	
Camp	14th ,,	13	
,,	15th ,,	18	Supplies not begun to be used till this evening.
,,	16th ,,	10¼	
Gulbasher	17th ,,	18	
Shahidoolla	18th ,,	23	Total 330½ miles. The last eleven marches being down the valley of the Karakash."

CHAPTER III.

HALT AT SHAHIDULLA—YAKUB KHAN, KASHGHAR ENVOY—SPECIAL COURIERS—ANNUAL YARKAND CARAVANS—PARTY PROCEEDS TO SANJU—KIRGHIZ AND YAKS—SANJU PASS—BULLOCK CARRIAGE—MIRZA BAHAUDIN—ABU-BAKR'S FORT—KILIAN KIRGHIZ—MISSION AND ENVOY REACH SANJU—KARGALIK—YARKAND—VISIT TO THE GOVERNOR: TO THE CITY—DRESS AND APPEARANCE OF THE PEOPLE—STREETS AND BAZAARS—MARKET DAY—HUNTING-EAGLES—BEGGARS—POPULATION—MISSION QUARTERS—SOLDIERS—CARTS.

THE Mission was under orders to halt on the frontier till joined by Yakub Khan Tora, the Kashghar Envoy to the Viceroy of India. Yakub Khan, after completing the preliminaries of the commercial treaty which he was sent to negotiate, proceeded to Constantinople, where it was arranged with the Sultan's government to declare Kashghar a protected state of Turkey, with Muhammad Yakub Khan (known as the Atalik Ghazi) as ruler, under the title of Amír. The Envoy found the formalities of the Sultan's court sadly against quick despatch of business, and his departure for the return journey was delayed considerably beyond his calculations and our plans. The progress of the camp from Rawal Pindi, where it was organised, was slow; the halts were long, pending definite orders, which depended entirely on the return of the Kashghar envoy. Our feeling of suspense during all that time of doubt was painful, and our delight was great when we were secured against bitter disappointment; for had the envoy not come back when he did, we would probably have lost for a time the opportunity of visiting Eastern Turkistan and exploring the Pamirs. Yakub Khan succeeded, however, by dint of good arrangements and hard travelling, in reaching Shahidulla on the 23d of October. We were overtaken on the 3d, at Tagar, in the Nubra valley, by Mulla Artuk, the envoy's special messenger to the Atalik, who also brought a letter from the same to Mr. Forsyth. The Mulla had travelled so far from Egypt in twenty-eight days, and reached Shahidulla, a distance of 177 miles farther on, over the high Susser, Karakoram, and Suget passes, on the 9th, six days later.

The distances done by these special couriers, riding the same horses day after day, is remarkable. Mulla Artuk, above mentioned, reached Shahidulla with the same horses that he took from our camp in Nubra. Haji Mehmet, another similar messenger, overtook me on the 24th, 36 miles beyond Shahidulla, riding direct from Aktagh, which he left the previous day, travelling 62 miles in twenty-nine hours, and crossing the high Suget and Sanju passes. He was despatched by Yakub Khan to announce to the Atalik his arrival at the frontier. The rate of travelling is of course greatly increased in the open country, and on the roads between the large towns, where posting-stations are established for rapid communication. The horses are urged to the utmost by the riders, whose exertions are largely stimulated by hope of reward and fear of punishment. A rapid journey is invariably rewarded, and delay is immediately noticed in a converse manner, no excuse being allowed. No feeling of "kismut" influences the messenger as he struggles hard, and spares neither himself nor horse in the endeavour to out-gallop all others and get a higher reward, though he acknowledges the "inevitable" in the issue if disappointing.

The annual caravans from Yarkand to Leh and India began to reach Shahidulla as we arrived, and we soon found that the pasture there was not sufficient to subsist our horses as well as theirs, nor was the food supply enough for the whole party to keep together till the Kashghar envoy should join. It was therefore arranged that a great portion of our camp should proceed to Sanju, five days' journey on in the inhabited country, where supplies were plentiful; and Captains Biddulph and Trotter, Dr. Stoliczka, and myself, accordingly left for that place on the 21st of October. Our Indian servants had at once occasion to regret the change from Tartar to Kirghiz, the former being patient and obliging to a degree, ever ready to do anything and everything for them, while the latter smilingly declined to assist in any way beyond preparing the yaks, regulating their loads, and driving the animals when laden. We crossed the Sanju pass (16,650 feet) on the 23d. It was deep with fresh snow, and here, for the third and last time during my journey, riding yaks were used. The yaks furnished on this occasion by the Kir-

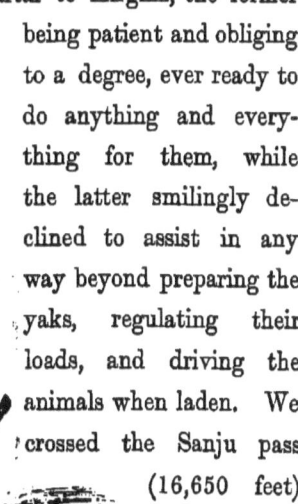
KIRGHIZ YOUTH.

ghiz appeared better movers than the Ladaki animals previously ridden. They were subject in a greater degree to control and guidance by the single rope attached to the nose ring, and were capable of being managed and urged by the rider with less difficulty than the similar Ladaki steed, which consents to carry its burden only under loud protest, and after much pulling and pushing at head and tail. After halting a day at the foot of the pass, to exchange the yak for bullock carriage, sent from the low country to meet us, we proceeded towards Sanju, and reached on the 27th. We met several caravans at the foot of the pass, all checked by the late heavy snow, which completely closed the way to them, unassisted by the Kirghiz and their yaks. These Kirghiz are the nomadic inhabitants of the Kilian hills, in the vicinity of Sanju, and came originally from the Sirikol district. The drivers with the new (bullock) transport were very different from the indolent independent Kirghiz. Though speaking Turki, a language utterly unknown to our camp servants, they contrived, in their extreme willingness to help, to understand how to make themselves useful in many ways; and the discouraging effect on our attendants of their first experience of the temper of the new people they were to be thrown among was thus soon removed.

After crossing the Sanju pass my party was joined by Mirza Bahaudin, from Shahidulla. He was one of the first officials sent from Yarkand to meet the Mission, and write the reports for Kashghar. He was, as far as I could gather, a secretary appointed direct by the Atalik to reside at Yarkand and keep him acquainted with all occurrences, in the manner practised in eastern governments from the earliest times. He

was a wise and discreet "mirza," full of information on many subjects, but very chary of imparting it. In part return for many complimentary attentions and civilities on his part, I made a flattering likeness of him in my sketch-book (which he was always examining with the utmost curiosity), which, while pretending indifference to for some time, he afterwards showed his decided approval of, by speaking of it in such a manner as to cause his admirers to come often and look at it.

The low state of the Sanju stream permitted us to pass down along it the whole way instead of taking the "Chu-chu" circuitous route, which is followed in summer when the stream is high. Winter had quite set in when we reached Turkistan, and the country was everywhere "burnt up," as the expression there is, with frost. The ruins of a stone fort and barrier wall are seen at the junction of the Chu-chu road with the main one. The story told in connection with the place is, that between three and four hundred years ago, Abu-Bakr, a ruler of Yarkand, when driven out by a successful rival, built this fort, and levied contributions from all passers by. He gave such trouble, and so defied all attempts to capture him or his fort, that at last a large reward was offered for his head, and his death was effected through the treachery of one of his adherents. His head was taken to Yarkand, and the body was buried on the banks of the Karakash, near the northern approach to the Sanju pass. We saw the "akoi" (white house) felt tents of the Kirghiz here and there in sheltered spots by the Sanju stream before reaching the cultivated and inhabited country lower down. A small present at a hamlet of these enabled me to obtain several "studies" for my sketch-book. When the first disinclination to "sit" was

F

overcome, and the suspicion at the unusual request was dissipated by seeing the work of the pencil, the head of the "Kosh" (families) hurried off the youngest and prettiest woman among the onlookers, re-appeared with her dressed in a gaudy flowered robe, with a baby in her arms, and introduced her as worthy of special notice. As a head-dress the Kirghiz women wear a white cloth rolled evenly, fold on fold, over a close-fitting red or other coloured cap with ear lappets, the whole finished off by passing the end of the turban over the ear-lappets and under the chin. The robes are of white and coloured cotton cloth, quilted with raw cotton for winter wear. The old Kirghiz grandmother wore a silver bangle on her right arm, and a silver "shawl-pin" to confine the inner robe close to the throat. This was the only occasion on which I observed jewellery worn by women in Eastern Turkistan. I found the whole party of women engaged in making felt. The dress of the Kirghiz men differs in no material manner from that of the settled inhabitants.

The head-quarters of the Mission, accompanied by the Kashghar envoy, reached Sanju on the 30th. A halt of two days was made to allow of Yakub Khan's heavy baggage coming up, especially the two mountain battery rifled guns

KIRGHIZ YOUNG WOMAN.

presented to the Atalik by the Khedive of Egypt, for the conveyance of which and other heavy cases several Bactrian

KIRGHIZ OLD WOMAN (GRANDMOTHER).

(double-humped) camels were waiting. We all left on the 2d of November, and reached the flourishing town of Kargalik on the 5th. Here we found such well-built, spacious, and comfortable quarters prepared for us, our followers, and horses, that in our extreme anxiety to proceed we feared these elaborate arrangements to mean detention and a lengthened stay. The carpeted rooms and cheery fires, in fireplaces with smokeless chimneys, were otherwise very enjoyable after our cold journey from Leh. Kargalik is situated on the main road from Yarkand to Guma and Khoten, and is the meeting point of the roads from Leh by the Sanju, Kilian, and Yangi Dawan passes, and from Tashkurgan, Sirikol, by the Tong route. The Chinese recognised the strategic importance of Kargalik, and had a fort there, now in ruins. The Hakim of Guma visited the Mission as it passed through a portion of his district between Sanju and Kargalik. In a present of game sent by him we saw for the first time the "Shaw" pheasant, which to the ordinary eye looks exactly like our own home bird. We heard of ibex on the heights above Sanju, but were unable to go out after them.

We reached the city of Yarkand on the 8th of November, and were remarkably well received by the people as well as by the officials. Yakub Khan, as the successful ambassador to India and Constantinople, received a warm welcome, and was made much of. We were met by the Governor's son at the head of a mounted guard, and by crowds of the townspeople mounted and dressed in holiday bright-coloured garments. Our escort of cavalry and infantry of the Punjab Guide Corps (numbering twenty-two) attracted attention by their neat appearance. The horses of the troopers had been well cared for on the journey over the Karakoram, and showed in good condition. We "mounted" the infantry soldiers from the first, and, looking after their own ponies, each man came to smarten his animal and riding equipment as carefully as if he had belonged to the cavalry branch of the service.

We visited Muhammad Yunas, the Dadkhwah (Governor, lit. "demander of justice") of Yarkand, the day after our arrival. Serjeant Rhind (our camp serjeant, who belonged to the 92d Highlanders) created a sensation by appearing in the full Highland costume of his kilted uniform. The Dadkhwah was courteous and kindly in his manner, and expressed much pleasure at again welcoming Mr. Forsyth to Yarkand. He seemed pleased with the presents given to him, among which was a large musical box, brought in playing "Come where my

TRAVELS IN TURKISTAN. 37

love lies dreaming." We found our robes of honour, signifying
high favour, awaiting us on return to the Mission residence, a
delicate piece of attention and consideration on the part of the
Dadkhwah. These robes are always of startling " thunder-and-

YARKAND OFFICIAL.

lightning" patterns; and had the custom been followed of
giving them at the time of our visit, and throwing them over

our shoulders as usual on such occasions, to be worn and exhibited in public on the way back, we would have presented an amusing if not absurd appearance, dressed in uniform as we were.

We were allowed to visit the city and go about the country as we chose, the only condition being that we should always be accompanied by one of the Governor's officials. This was perfectly reasonable, and was easily explained as necessary for several reasons, without mentioning the real object. We rode through the town and its bazaars on the day following our visit to the Governor. No restrictions had been placed on the appearance of females in the streets, as was done at the time of Mr. Forsyth's first mission in 1870; and in their eager curiosity to see us, we had many opportunities of studying ladies' " winter fashions " in Yarkand. I say "winter fashions," because on our return from the Oxus in May, we found a thorough revolution in ladies' dress, extending to hats and shoes. In winter the head covering consists of an exaggerated "rink" fur cap, generally made of black lamb's wool, with a top trim-

YARKAND WOMAN.

ming of otter fur, and a crown of coloured silk or cotton cloth. This is worn over a large square of white muslin which hangs down the back, and is sometimes brought over the shoulders and tied in front. I have seen it held by the teeth to act as a pretence for a veil. The hair is generally plaited in two long tails, but is at times worn loose in ringlets. The robes are long and ample, and cut straight; the outer one showing by the chevrons across the chest whether the wearer is married or not, the chevrons being the distinguishing mark of a wife. Long leather or embroidered coloured cloth boots, with high heels, complete the costume. The outer robes are made of thick strong cotton cloth, wadded with the raw material, and of all colours and patterns, from the brightest to the quietest. The chevrons are always of a colour to contrast with that of the robe. The colours most in vogue with the mass are grey, chocolate, dark green, and blue. The inner robes are generally white, with red chevrons. On holiday occasions they show in dresses of Khoten and Andijani silk, with large Chinese-like patterns on bright grounds, and conspicuous borders and linings, with embroidered cloth boots, neatly trimmed with floss silk rosettes, all in good keeping with the prevailing colour. The inner robes on such occasions are also of bright colours. The children have similar attention and taste displayed in their dress on fête days, and some were seen with coloured silk bows and bands, and equally neat shoes. The superior class wear fur-lined silk robes, and caps made entirely of the valuable Siberian otter fur, a skin of which sells there at nine " tillas," equivalent to £5. No jewellery appears to be worn.

The "height of fashion" is to connect the eyebrows straight across, increase the hair plaits to the utmost that can possibly be thought natural (when the wearer has not abundant locks), and give colour to the cheeks by artificial means.

The horn-shaped head-dress mentioned by Shaw is occasionally seen. The tunic, of light muslin, sometimes thrown over it, is simply a light summer dress worn with it as a wrapper. The veil is worn, but is seldom used. It is thrown coquettishly back over the cap, or put up under it. The custom used to be for the women to go about unveiled, but under the Atalik's severe application of Muhammadan law this is now forbidden, and on the approach of the "Kazi" (religious magistrate) on his rounds, there is always a general rush among the women in the streets to escape from his observation, or to get out and pull down their veils. At first when we used to ride through the city, the Yuzbashi or other attendant official would ride ahead, and call to the women to veil before the strangers, but latterly they ceased this, and our approach caused no alarm or hurried escape.

YARKAND WOMAN.

The ordinary dress of the men is a close-fitting cap lined with lamb's wool or fur, turned up all round at the bottom, the same style of robe as the women, but confined at the waist by a cotton girdle, and long plain leather riding boots, with felt stockings. The better class wear the high "tilpak" cap, lined with otter or other expensive fur, and fur-lined robes. Turbans are also worn with or without the fur cap, but they are an article of luxury not often within the reach of the lower class. For the latter, sheepskin, with the wool attached, is the universal warm material for winter caps and coats, and it, with felt and cotton coverlets, forms the bedding of all classes.

Fair complexions and black hair prevail. In figure both men and women are middle sized, strong, and robust. The women are often rather handsome, with fresh-coloured pleasant faces, and neat small feet. As a people they are of a merry, happy disposition, fond of amusement, music, and dancing, but under the present priestly rule they are considerably restricted in these pleasures.

The streets of Yarkand city present a busy, cheerful appearance. Everything is well ordered and arranged. Separate bazaars, some of them covered, are appointed for the sale of different kinds of merchandise and manufactures; and loud-voiced hawkers, with trays of small wares, pie-men with barrows, and market gardeners carrying baskets in the Indian "banghy" fashion, suspended from a supple pole laid over the shoulders, go about from place to place. Water-carriers also carry water buckets in the same "banghy" fashion, as well as in one long deep bucket with a pole passed through the handles, resting on the shoulders of two men. Whenever we stopped at a shop to purchase, or make inquiry as to cost, the moderate prices asked of the native buyers were at once raised extravagantly high, and a crowd immediately collected to see the "Firangi." This was the term by which we were known and spoken of by the people at first, but it was not used in an offensive sense as is sometimes supposed to be the case in India.

All Europeans are known in Turkistan as "Firangi." In Wakhan, where we were in high favour with all the people, an old man who remembered Wood, the famous traveller, spoke of him in the most respectful manner after he was informed of his being a countryman of ours, as "Firangi." We always found the crowds, through which we had to press our way on horseback, respectful and good humoured to a degree.

Every town has its one weekly market day, when the people of the surrounding country flock in to buy and sell. Yarkand is crowded to excess on its market day. Our first visit to this weekly gathering drew a great following of inquisitive villagers wherever we appeared. On such days the shops do a brisk trade, and the cries of rival vendors in praise of their goods are deafening and unceasing. The Chinese cooks shout out the delights of their "made" dishes, ready to be served up hot and steaming in pottery bowls at the clean well-scrubbed tables inside their tidy restaurants. Horses and cattle, sheep and goats, are there sold in their different market places outside the city walls. The gallows, described by Mr. Shaw as occupying a very conspicuous place in the city when he made his first adventurous visit in 1868, now stands in a corner of the sheep market. Women are to be seen riding to market in "cavalier" fashion, and making their purchases in a thoroughly businesslike manner. The sex holds a much more honourable position in the household in Turkistan than in India.

We saw the "burgut" (mentioned by Marco Polo and Atkinson), hunting golden eagle, at Yarkand for the first time. A gazelle, killed by trained eagles, was sent to us, and on our expressing a desire to see some sport with these birds, seven were sent out to meet us at some likely ground beyond the city. We were not fortunate enough to find any large game, and two

STREET SCENE YARKAND

"flights" at heron proved unsuccessful. Captain Biddulph, however, had some sport with them during a trip he made from Kashghar to Marulbashi, which I shall mention farther on in my narrative, and illustrate with drawings made from the life on the occasion now noted, and Captain Biddulph's personal description of the manner in which the bird strikes and seizes its prey. On returning from our morning's ride with the eagles, we fell in with a large party of the town's people playing at "oghlak," the game on horseback so well described in Shaw's *Yarkand*. Some of us joined in it with the attendant officials, who rode well, and greatly enjoyed the fast and furious fun.

Beggars are a recognised and regular institution in Yarkand, forming quite a professional body. Beggars marry there, and the children grow up to follow their parents' example. Beggars ride in their travels through the country with bells attached to the horses' necks, to draw attention to the profession of the rider, and the fact that alms are expected. This privileged class do not beg in the usual manner, but loudly demand charity in the name of "Allah," as a religious obligation due to them, addressing the passers-by with cries of "Hakk, hakk," meaning "the rights, the dues," and giving thanks by the usual stroking of the beard with both hands, and the "Alla-ho-akbar." It is amusing to see the female beggars gravely making the same beard-stroking gesture. But while the characteristic religious government of the "Atalik Ghazi" thus tolerates mendicants as a professional body, the able-bodied find no place in it, and a "sturdy beggar" is never seen. Various causes combine to remove such to an active and useful life, as soldiers or servants. Vagrancy is not permitted; all vagabonds and men unable to give a good account of themselves, are, if capable of service, pressed into the ranks of the army.

The city walls of Yarkand are well kept up, and small guards hold its gateways. The space enclosed by the walls is great, a fact which appears hitherto to have had a misleading effect in calculating the number of inhabitants. The accounts previously given of the population were based on the supposition that there was little open space or garden ground within the city wall, but this is now known to be incorrect. We estimated the population at 40,000.

During our stay we occupied the quarters which were assigned to Mr. Forsyth on his first visit in 1870. These were situated within the "Yangi-Shahr," or fortified cantonment outside the city, where the Governor and his officials reside. The Dadkhwah, Muhammad Yunas, is the second dignitary in the kingdom, and keeps up considerable state. His guards were the first of the regular troops we saw. They are composed of a great mixture of classes and nationalities. A party of five sent to us to be "pictured" consisted of two Tashkendis, one Khokandi, one Kashgari, and one Yarkandi. His artillery guard were the only soldiers with whom uniform was attempted. They serve odd pieces of ordnance parked near the Governor's "urda" (palace), besides long wall pieces called "taifu," which they also carry and use in the field.

On the 25th of November the cases and packages containing the presents for the Amír, and our heavy baggage, were despatched to Kashghar in the excellent light carts of the country. These carts are said to have been introduced by the Chinese; they carry about 16 cwt., and are dragged by four horses, of which one is in the shafts and three in front. Only the wheeler and near leader have driving-reins, the others in front being connected with the latter by coupling-reins. The leaders' traces run from their collars to the body of the cart

CAPTAIN AND MURSHID OF THE YARKAND GOVERNOR'S GUARD

underneath, and are supported by wooden hoops suspended to both ends of the shafts. These carts are of great breadth between the wheels, and remarkably easy of draught. The usual travelling complement of horses is four, harnessed as already mentioned, but for ordinary work or short distances they are often used with one horse, and sometimes with two in tandem fashion. I have even seen four leaders to one in the shafts, but the extra horse appeared to be undergoing training with steady companions. The field artillery guns at Kashghar are harnessed with three horses unicorn fashion.

A WOMAN OF SANJU.

CHAPTER IV.

DEPARTURE FOR KASHGHAR—POST HOUSES—COMMANDANT OF YANGI-HISSAR FORT—GUNS CARRIED BY ALL OFFICIALS—YANGI-HISSAR—KASHGHAR—RECEPTION BY THE ATALIK—CITY—COTTON MANUFACTURES—EXPORT TRADE—SILK—WOOL—CHINESE AND TUNGANIS — DOMESTIC SLAVES — SKATING — MECHANICS AND ARTISANS.

WE were entertained by the Dadkhwah on the 27th with a wonderful effort of cookery in countless dishes, prepared in the Chinese fashion, after which we said good-bye to our kind host, and took our departure for Kashghar the following day. We travelled by the same road that Messrs. Shaw and Hayward went by in 1868, and which has been fully described by them. Pheasants and gazelles were seen on the way, but our daily journeys were too long to allow of sport. We made five stages to Kashghar, of 25, 30, 32, 22, and 15 miles respectively, halting two days at Yangi-Hissar. The staging houses along the road had been prepared for our reception, and we found in the blue, red, and white "posts" comfortable accommodation, very different from what we would have had in our tents in the severe cold then prevailing. Robat is the Turki for posthouse, and on the Yarkand-Kashghar road, Kok, Ak, and Kizil Robat are met with;—the blue, white, and red "posts," so called from local peculiarities.

Khul Muhammad, Pansad-Bashi (head of 500), Commandant of the Yangi-Hissar fort, met the Mission half-way from

Yarkand, and conducted us to Ak-Robat, a posting stage in the desert, where we were welcomed with a hot breakfast. The Commandant was accompanied by a well-mounted and equipped guard of nineteen men, armed with percussion-lock rifles, manufactured in Kashghar after an obsolete Euro-

KHUL MUHAMMAD.

pean army pattern. The men were uniformly dressed in yellow tanned leather long coats and wide trousers, edged with fur. They waited on us at breakfast, as all such guards and attendants do, spreading the "dastar-khwan" cloth, and handing in the dishes in a noiseless and ready manner. Khul Muhammad, Bai Baba, a strikingly good-looking, fair-haired Khokandi officer with him, and the "Usher of the white rod," in attendance on the Mission during the stay at Yangi-Hissar, all gave me opportunities of sketching them in

BAI BABA.

my pocket-book. A peeled willow wand is the mark of special duty, and is often seen carried by mounted couriers as well as by subordinate officials on ceremonial occasions. Every official who bears arms, from the highest to the lowest, carries a gun or rifle, and never moves out on important duty or public business without it. Yakub Khan, the Atalik's nephew, and Kashghar envoy, who returned with us, was the only exception I observed to this rule; and though he appeared without the usual gun, he carried at his belt, in the prevailing fashion, powder and ball bags and "priming" horn, with numerous other gun appliances and appendages. I saw Beg-Kuli-Beg, the Amír's eldest son, ride past the Mission residence at Kashghar, with Niaz Beg, the governor of Khoten, both carrying guns slung over their shoulders in the ordinary manner, and Nubbi Buksh, the principal military commander, who showed the troops to us there, bore a double-barrelled rifle.

The view on approaching Yangi-Hissar is very pretty. The town was crowded with people assembled to see us pass. It has a long covered bazaar with numerous busy shops, and looks as if it were the centre of a thriving local trade. A lofty gallows fitted for three occupies a conspicuous place at one end of the town. The fort is built on the usual Chinese rectangular plan with projecting towers, and ditch and glacis; it appears comparatively new, and is said to be well garrisoned and provided.

We reached Kashghar on the 4th of December. Mirza Ahmed Kush-Begi, formerly governor of Tashkend under the Khokand government, and now holding high rank at the Atalik's court, met the Mission some distance off for the usual "istikbal" (honourable reception), and conducted us to the "Elchi Khana," a very commodious set of quarters opposite the entrance to the Atalik's fortified palace (the Yangi-Shahr or military cantonment of Kashghar). Here was found comfort-

H

able accommodation for the whole party, including the escort, servants, and followers. Good stabling was provided for the riding horses, and the pack animals were well sheltered behind the high protecting walls of the enclosure. Ihrar Khan Tora, who had visited India some years before as envoy from Kashghar, was appointed Mihmandar (in charge of guests), with the royal instructions to see that the "king's guests" should want for nothing. We were summoned by the Atalik to pay him a private visit on the day of our arrival. A large crowd had assembled to see us come, and remained all day about the place to see us again when we issued to make our visit. We were received by the Atalik in the most friendly manner, indicative at once of the perfect honour and safety in which our stay there was made throughout the winter, and as long as we were in Kashghar territory. Nothing else was to be expected considering the high auspices under which we proceeded there, and the uniformly kindly disposition which the Atalik Ghazi has always shown towards Europeans.

Etiquette forbade our visiting the city till our formal reception by the Atalik, and the presentation of her Majesty the Queen's and the Viceroy's letters had taken place. The Atalik's absence on a short pilgrimage to a saintly shrine in the neighbourhood delayed this till the 11th, when all was done with the utmost ceremony and display. We went to the city on the 12th, and the inhabitants then saw Europeans for the first time within its walls. Alish Beg, the Dadkhwah of Kashghar, entertained us at a bewildering banquet of over one hundred dishes, and for the more convenient attention to which he had caused tables and chairs to be made for our especial use. We had also found tables and chairs in our well-carpeted rooms in the Elchi

Khana, showing how all our wants and ways had been considered and provided for. A guard of Tunganis with "taifu" wall pieces held the city gate by which we entered.

The city of Kashghar is not so large as that of Yarkand, being three miles in circumference, while the latter is three and a half. Both are surrounded by mud walls of great thickness, with many projecting square towers. Both towns are built entirely of mud, and have no pretensions whatever to anything remarkable in architecture. Two branches of the "Kizil Su," or Kashghar river, flow past the city, the one on the north and the other on the south, meeting at a short distance below. Both of these branches are crossed by well-constructed wooden bridges. Kashghar is the terminus of a considerable trade with the Russian possessions extending from Tashkend to Kuldja.

The manufactures of the country are confined chiefly to silk and cotton, both of which are abundantly produced in it. The silk mainly comes from Khoten, where it is worked up by itself, and also mixed with cotton, into a variety of fabrics for home use and foreign export. The stout cotton cloths of Eastern Turkistan are well known for their durability in the markets of Badakhshan and Russian Turkistan beyond the Tian Shan; and there is a steady export trade in them from Kashghar, Yarkand, and Khoten. The only foreign cotton goods that find a sale in Eastern Turkistan are the fine kinds, and muslin, chintzes, and prints, the manufacture of which is not yet understood, but the demand for these is limited by being beyond the means of the mass of the population. This fact should, I think, settle the question of any important market in that part of Central Asia for Manchester goods.

The raw silk of Khoten is coarse and inferior, simply from

want of skill and care in its preparation. The absence of a better market than the country itself affords is against any change at present, but the opening of a direct trade with India by the easy route I have mentioned would soon correct this, and bring about an improvement, similar to what is now being effected with Kashmir silk, which promises fair to equal yet the good produce of other countries. This trade between Khoten and India could be carried on by an extension of the operations of the present shawl wool traders who visit the Rudok districts annually, with flocks of load-carrying sheep, taking rice, flour, coarse cloths, and other articles to barter for the "pushm" of the shawl goat. The silk of Khokand is superior to that of Khoten, and it again is excelled by that of Bokhara, which commands the highest price in the Indian market. With direct routes and more freedom of action to merchants in Eastern Turkistan, India might compete with China in silk as she is now doing in tea. The Khokand trade, of course, would be subject to Russian influence.

Felt and carpets are the only woollen fabrics made in Eastern Turkistan, except in the remote corner of Sirikol, where a rough "homespun" is produced for domestic use. Foreign cloths are imported to Eastern Turkistan, and sold at a high price principally to the upper class. There is a vast consumption of sheep in the country by its great meat-eating population, and the skins, with wool attached, are worked up into coats, caps, and bedding, as I have already told. In winter the sheepskin forms the covering of the labouring people night and day. Khoten and Kogiar, to the south of Yarkand, are famous for their superior felts.

Mention has been made of the inhabitants of the country

about Lop Nor wearing "clothes made of the bark of trees." I observed one of the Kashghari officials who accompanied me to the Tian Shan wearing a robe made of something very like linen duck, or fine canvas, and on asking concerning it, he said that he got the cloth at Aksu, and that it came from Lop, where it was made and used by the people. This would seem to point to flax plants being the "trees" spoken of as furnishing in their bark material for clothes.

A considerable number of pure Chinese are to be seen at Kashghar and Yarkand. Almost all, with the exception of those serving in the army, are in poor circumstances, as artizans and menial servants, or as street hawkers, the last resource of the old and worn out. The late successive revolutions and Muhammadan risings, which ended in the firm establishment of the

KASSIM AKHUN, ALIAS CHAWLIANG KHWAITANG.

present sovereignty, reduced the Chinese, who saved their lives by embracing the faith of the conquerors, to poverty and slavery. All these proselytes had to abandon their Chinese names and take the Muhammadan ones given by the triumphant Mullas. One of them, a small shopkeeper in Yarkand, used to frequent our quarters there with Chinese curiosities for sale. He spoke sorrowfully of the change by which he lost his old name of Chawliang Khwaitang, and his pigtail, when told that he was thenceforth Kassim Akhun, a true believer. Seeing a chance of profitable sale for old china, he offered to show a very rare piece, but explained that secrecy was absolutely necessary in the transaction, in order to conceal his possession of such a costly article as it was. The simple fellow made his appearance the following evening, and produced most cautiously from under his capacious robe a coarse European earthenware figure of a sheep, with a movable top, such as is seen as an ornament on a cottage mantelpiece. The original price was probably one shilling, but the owner valued it at about two pounds sterling. We left him in undisturbed possession of his treasure, which he firmly believed in, regarding our account of its Western manufacture as an invention with the object of depreciating its value. Tunganis are also seen in the position of slaves, probably captives brought by returning warriors from the Eastern campaigns about Turfan, and permitted to be kept as household servants. Under the Atalik, slavery is forbidden by law, but this practically only extends to public traffic. Slavery in the modified form of domestic bondage still exists, but only as a foreign institution, in which the mass of the population have no share or interest.

Several of our party had come provided with skates, and

these were soon put in requisition, to the surprise and astonishment of the people, who had never seen the like before. Skating is known, though not practised, in Khokand. It has probably been seen by many of the inhabitants in the neighbouring Russian cantonments. It was a very popular amusement with us, and one which some of our escort tried hard to learn how to enjoy. The most perfect imitations of our skates were produced for us in the Atalik's workshops, and an attempt was made to induce the courtiers to take to the amusement. Two were found willing to try, but the awkward contortions and struggles of a beginner were too much in opposition to the solemn and serious deportment of the court, and after the first attempt the exercise was condemned as "undignified and ridiculous." We continued to indulge in it, however, to our own thorough enjoyment, and the amusement of the spectators, who sometimes regarded an occasional rare good fall at full-power speed as a part of the exercise, and loudly expressed their admiration of the performance.

Many of the mechanics and artizans employed in the Atalik's workshops are said to be Hindustanis and foreigners. Among the presents to the Atalik were sewing machines, one of which, a highly ornamental one, was broken in transit, and on inquiry as to the possibility of repair at Kashghar, a Khokandi was sent, who not only did all that was required, but also showed perfect acquaintance with the working of the machine. He told me that he gained his knowledge at Tashkend. We took up steam and other useful models, which, however, did not excite much interest. The electric telegraph, which I erected and worked with Captain Biddulph, attracted little or no attention, and the proposal to extend the wire into the Atalik's palace was not received in a manner to encourage its taking a practical form. The galvanic battery and wheel of life, as usual, proved most popular.

USHER OF THE WHITE ROD.

CHAPTER V.

DEPARTURE FOR THE TIAN SHAN—ARTUSH VALLEY AND STREAM—RUSSIAN MERCHANTS—TOYAN VALLEY AND STREAM—FORTS OF THE CHAKMAK DEFILE—CARAVAN ROUTE—OLD VOLCANO—*OVIS POLI* AND BLACK IBEX—RUSSIAN KAZAKS AND KARA KIRGHIZ—HERDS OF PONIES—MANNER OF HUNTING *OVIS POLI*—KIRGHIZ SOLDIERS AND SPORTSMEN—CHADIR KUL LAKE—WATERSHED—TIAN SHAN RANGE—SEVERE COLD—CAPTAIN TROTTER'S WORK—STRICT CHURCH DISCIPLINE—EXCAVATED ROOMS AT ARTUSH.

BLACK IBEX.

THE Envoy, Mr. Forsyth, having obtained permission from the Mission to visit the Chadir-Kul lake, on the Tian Shan plateau, lying to the north of Kashghar, Dr. Stoliczka, Captain Trotter, and myself, left for that place on the 31st of December. We were asked by the local authorities to trust entirely to their hospitality for tents, food, and baggage animals, and accordingly as "guests" were obliged to accommodate ourselves to their arrangements. We thus found our roving propensities considerably restricted. The official appointed to accompany us did not share our anticipations of pleasure in visiting the Tian Shan highlands, and could not understand our desire to leave the comfortable quarters in Kashghar and travel in the mountains in the severe Arctic cold then prevailing there. Our intention, at starting, was to visit both the Torugat and Terekty passes over the southern crest of the Tian Shan, but we were obliged to content ourselves with the trip to Chadir-Kul over the former, and return, leaving the latter unvisited.

Our first day's journey was to Bezakh, twenty-six miles from Yangi-Shahr, Kashghar, a village in the upper Artush district. The road lay in a northerly direction past the city of Kashghar, and through about four miles of gardens and fields to an open stony plain, leading by a gentle rising slope to a small spur from a low range of hills running from west to east, and through a gap in which the river Artush has forced its way. The road passes along the river bed through the range, and crosses to the north bank, there reaching the valley of Artush, a broad and far-extending fertile plain, studded with villages and hamlets, showing signs of thriving population and careful farming. This well-irrigated and closely-cultivated valley is well watered by never-failing streams from the Tian Shan and Terek ranges, and produces wonderfully rich and abundant harvests. We passed here two large camel caravans coming from Vernoe (Almati) to Kashghar with Russian goods, of which cast-iron cooking pots formed a considerable portion. These Russian iron vessels are in general use throughout Eastern Turkistan, and among the Kirghiz. The caravans take back the thick durable cotton cloths which form the staple article of the Kashghar export trade. We were accommodated for the night in the house of the Bai (head) of the village, who, unfortunately for us, was absent, otherwise we would probably not have suffered from a short supply of food as we did that night, owing to hasty arrangements, and possibly the desire of our attendant official to magnify difficulties and discomforts, so as to induce compliance with his wish for early return.

We continued our journey the following day in a westerly direction for three miles across the Artush valley to the mouth of the Toyan valley and stream, up which we proceeded to Chung Terek (big poplars), a distance of twenty miles. The Toyan stream, which flows from the Torugat pass, divides into two branches where it debouches into the plains in the Artush valley; the upper one flows nearly due east, and is the principal source of irrigation in this fertile plain. The south or main branch flows south-east into the river Artush, which is said to rise in the Terek mountains on the road to Khokand.

On entering the Toyan valley, here about two miles wide, we may be said to have fairly entered the Tian Shan mountains. The ridge we had crossed on the previous day's journey (and which at its highest point is only a few hundred feet above the plain) is rather an isolated ridge than a portion of the main range. In marching up this open valley we had in view the rough serrated edges of the Ming-yol hill, a prominent object in the panoramic view from the roof of the Embassy buildings in Kashghar, from which it has the appearance of a large isolated hill. On going partially round it, however, it appeared to be only the end of a long ridge of nearly uniform height, running in a direction a little north of west, towards the angle formed by the junction of the Tian Shan with the Alai range.

In continuing our march up the valley, we saw in front, at a distance however of only a few miles, some snowy peaks, the same that are visible from Kashghar, behind the Artush range, and which thence appear to be peaks of the main range running south of the Chadir-Kul. They are not so, however, but form a lower range of hills running nearly parallel to the main range, *i.e.* from west to east. At six miles from the Artush is the Khitai (Chinese) or Tessik-tash Karawal (guard-house), a little square fort used as a customs post, and now held by a small party of Kashghar troops. This was the most advanced post in this direction held by the Chinese during their occupation of the country.

Chung Terek is a most picturesque spot, and in summer the scenery there must be singularly beautiful. The river banks at some places below Chung Terek have a height of fully 200 feet, and are cut by rivulets into remarkably regular-looking pillars and turrets, presenting the appearance of imitation by nature of human art. We saw Kirghiz scattered over the whole valley, located wherever grazing was available for their flocks and herds. Many of their "akoi" hamlets show signs of settled habitation in patches of irrigated and cultivated ground, which are probably attended by the family elders when the annual summer move to the high pasture lands takes place.

Leaving Chung Terek on the third day, we reached the Chakmak forts, twenty-one miles up the Toyan, over a gentle but regular ascent the whole way. About two miles above Chung Terek the valley suddenly narrows, and continues confined between precipitous hills for about twenty miles. At ten miles from the commencement of this defile is the fort of Mirza Terek, a carefully constructed work which could give a great deal of trouble to an enemy advancing from the north; both here and at Chakmak, nine miles farther up the stream, the overhanging

VIEW IN THE TO-UN VALLEY NEAR CHUNG PEEN, TIAN SHAN — LOOKING

heights are so precipitous and inaccessible that it would be almost impossible for the enemy to effect a lodgment in them. The fort itself sweeps the whole of the approach, in addition to which an extended curtain wall, secured against view and enfilade, affords a strong flank defence. The Chakmak fort is a place of remarkable strength, its natural advantages having been greatly increased by skilfully placed works, and well selected lines of defence. These fortifications are said to have been designed and built four years ago by Beg-Kuli-Beg, the eldest son of the Atalik. Mahmud Beg, the "Toksabai" (Lord of the Standard) in command, welcomed us kindly and treated us most hospitably, accommodating us in comfortable quarters inside the fort, a pleasant change from the small, tattered Kirghiz felt tent, admitting a distressing amount of cold, in which we had passed the previous night.

We continued in the same general north-west direction on the fourth day, passing the Suyuk Karawal, eight miles up the Toyan, where the Suyuk stream joins, flowing from the pass of the same name. The Suyuk pass, distant thence about two days' journey, is little more than a footpath, and is not fit for horses; but the road from the Torugat pass, about thirty miles to the north, is used by laden camels, and is open throughout the year. The Torugat is the most used caravan route from the north to eastern Turkistan. The road is good all the way, and the only difficulties are where it crosses the stream. In winter the stream is, as we found it, partially frozen over for almost its entire length. The slope from the Artush valley, height about 5300 feet, to the Torugat pass, 12,760 feet, a distance of eighty miles, is tolerably uniform throughout, and gives therefore a regular rise of about 100 feet per mile.

On leaving Chakmak our conductor tried to deter us from

going on by warnings about the cold, and only took us a distance of ten miles that day, to Gulja-bashi, a spot in a sheltered valley with abundant pasturage and bush fuel. Our party was there joined by three Yuzbashis and a Kirghiz guard from the Chakmak garrison. The following day we made a march of fifteen miles to Torugat-bela, an interesting road, as after passing through volcanic rocks we came to a place where the banks, rising to many hundreds of feet in perpendicular height, bore unmistakable signs of being the crater of an extinct volcano. Our geologist, Dr. Stoliczka, who had previously expressed his belief in the existence of an old volcano in this quarter, was of course delighted. Sir Henry Rawlinson, the President of the Royal Geographical Society of England, in addressing the meeting of the 15th June 1874, said with reference to this that the discovery of an extinct crater on the outer skirts of the Tian Shan was a most important addition to our knowledge of the physical geography of the region, confirming, as it did, what the great Humboldt always maintained with regard to the Tian Shan, but what the Russian geographers have recently disputed.

We saw on this day's journey, for the first time, the "*Ovis poli*," hitherto regarded as a half mythical animal. On leaving the road and wandering over the grass-covered undulating hills and long sloping flats to the west, we saw several large flocks of this gigantic wild sheep, but were not fortunate enough to shoot any. One of our party, in his intense eagerness to be the envied "first" to bag a specimen, undertook a long and slow stalk round the summit of a ridge about 14,000 feet high, and was frost-bitten on the fingers from the cold contact of the rifle barrel before he got the chance of the shot, which he missed. The thermometer marked 26° below zero that night outside, and 8½° below zero inside our felt tent, pitched in the sheltered ground of Torugat-bela some distance below. The Torugat-bela pastures were occupied by Kara Kirghiz and Kazaks from the Narin valley, who come over every year from the Russian side with about 5000 ponies, for winter grazing on the southern slopes of the pass, and pay revenue while there to Kashghar. We saw great numbers of their stout well-made ponies all about. Both they and the men look enduring and active, and they must be hardy to a degree to stand as they do the chilling bitter wind of these heights in mid-winter.

The camp halted at the foot of the pass on the 5th January, and we went about twelve miles towards the west to look out for *Ovis poli*, of which we saw several large flocks, one numbering as many as eighty-five. We found them on open ground on the flat-topped spurs and rounded hills, but when alarmed they took to precipitous rocks as easily and confidently as ibex. I saw a black ibex, which I stalked till I was nearly frozen, but without getting a shot. Previous to this, not wishing to return empty-handed to camp, I had sent off two of my attendant mounted Kirghiz to try for *Ovis poli*, and they rejoined me on my way back with a fine ram. Finding that I had been unsuccessful, they pressed me hard to allow them to say that the "kill" was mine! Late in the evening another party of our Kirghiz escort returned with two *Ovis poli*, a female and a young male. We obtained in these an excellent supply of meat for our camp. This "mountain mutton" was good and pleasant to the taste, with a slight flavour of venison.

The nature of the country admits of the *Ovis poli* and the ibex even, when they come down to feed on the low ground as I saw, being stalked, followed, or met by the sportsman riding mounted on a trusty pony. With rifle slung, and accompanied by a couple of mounted Kirghiz, he wanders along, always approaching a ridge very carefully and peering cautiously over the edge. If game be seen the guides are consulted, and an understanding as to the course to be followed is arrived at. If the ground is very open it will probably be necessary to dismount and stalk in the ordinary manner, with all the science and care requisite on such occasions. If, however, as is often the case, in going along a broad open valley, a flock is seen to disappear behind a ridge perhaps a mile off, as hard a pace as the ground will admit of in the ponies carries up to a stalking point selected by the Kirghiz. The advantage of this sport lies in the excitement of the gallop, and the stalk as well, and the great extent of ground that can be covered in a day.

A number of the soldiers in the Chakmak command are Kipchaks, and Chirik, Alai, and Andijani Kirghiz. Mounted on the sturdy ponies for which the country is famous, good shots, and knowing thoroughly the surrounding country, they are admirably fitted for "scouting" and mounted infantry purposes. In the present time of peace they keep their ponies, hands, and eyes, in capital training, in hunting the *Ovis poli* and the ibex. We heard of about one hundred *Ovis poli* and ibex shot by the Kirghiz soldiers of the neighbouring parts, having been distributed on one occasion by the Atalik amongst the poor of the city of Kashghar during our stay there; and we were shown in the Chakmak fort the frozen carcases of about fifty *Ovis poli* and black ibex stored as part of the winter food supply for the garrison, all shot by the Kirghiz belonging to it.

On the 6th we went to the Chadir-Kul lake and back to camp, a ride of about thirty-two miles. Starting early in the morning, with the thermometer several degrees below zero, we rode about thirteen miles to the pass, a gentle ascent up the valley till

within a mile of the crest, when the rise, though still very easy, is somewhat steeper (about 400 feet in the last mile). We had a lovely day for the trip, and Captain Trotter was able to carry on his work right up to the pass, which he made to be 12,760 feet. On reaching the pass we did not come at once, as we had expected, into view of the lake, but had to go along a spur for about three miles in a northerly direction, when we burst suddenly into full view of the lake, and a perfect forest of peaks beyond extending from west to east. We were here about thirty-two miles from the Russian fort of Narin, by the Tash Robat pass, which lay immediately opposite us.

The lake lies east and west, and according to Russian accounts its elevation is 11,050 feet above sea-level, the length 14 miles, average breadth 6, depth inconsiderable, and water brackish. It has no outlet: it rises with the melting of the snow, and falls in the dry season. The plateau in which it lies extends towards the east into the Aksai table-land, where the Aksai stream rises, and flowing eastward, joins the Kashghar river below Aksu. The opening to the west leads towards the source of the Arpa, which finds its way into the Jaxartes (Sir). When we saw it, the lake was frozen and covered with snow, which made it difficult to distinguish between it and the nearly level plain by which it is surrounded, and which was covered with a white saline efflorescence.

Looking from our elevated position above the lake, there appeared to be two ranges of mountains,—the Torugat, on a spur of which we were standing, and the Tashrobat, on the opposite side of the lake. Both are portions of the Tian Shan range, which westward, like the Karakoram eastward, seems to lose its identity, and merges into several comparatively unimportant

K

minor chains, of which it is impossible to say which is the main one. Hence there is some difficulty in defining the watershed, and consequently the boundary between Russia and Kashghar. The general run of the Torugat range is from west to east; the peaks also decrease in height as the range approaches the pass: the highest within a few miles of it being about 15,000 feet; others, away to the west, being apparently 2000 feet or more higher. East of the pass, again, the hills are still lower, but it was impossible to judge of their general direction, though, from the Russian maps, it would appear to be south-east. We had hoped to cross the high undulating lands eastward to the Terekty pass, thirty or thirty-five miles distant, but the officials seemed to think we had seen enough, and we had to return to Kashghar.

Notwithstanding the intensity of the cold, Captain Trotter carried on his special work successfully throughout the journey. He had to take star observations, with the thermometer standing at 10° below zero, a bitter wind blowing, and no shelter available. To Captain Trotter belongs the distinction of being the first to carry the scientific survey of England across that of Russia in the East; the road from Kashghar to the crest of the Tian Shan being a link in the chain across Asia which is now common to both.

Many of the Kashghari servants slept out in the open by the horses, and appeared none the worse of the exposure. We were particularly struck with the excellent church discipline kept up by our Muhammadan hosts, who regularly intoned the call to prayers, and assembled outside the tents in obedience to it, at break of day, in a temperature of 25° below zero. Our Indian Muhammadan servants made no pretence of such extreme piety in that severe climate.

On the return journey we saw Kirghiz near Chakmak loading camels with blocks of ice cut in the Toyan, for transport up a side valley, where they were located with their flocks, their supply of water being thus obtained till the approach of warm weather releases the frost-bound springs. In leaving the Artush valley, we observed high up in the vertical face of the ridge, where the stream cuts its way through towards the Kashghar plain, three excavated chambers, each with an inner apartment behind. The only history of these excavations I could obtain was, that some eighty years ago the Chinese Amban (Governor), of Kashghar had a daughter so surpassingly lovely that all his friends and neighbours wished to marry her, and his enemies strove to steal her. The Amban idolised his daughter, and fearing to lose her had these chambers made and sumptuously fitted for her reception. An enemy desiring to do him the utmost injury tried to poison the food which used to be let down to her from the summit of the precipice; and the Amban after that, in suspicion of all prepared food, subsisted her on grapes. A wasp concealed in the grapes stung the beauty in the throat, and caused her death.

KIRGHIZ SOLDIERS AND PONIES.

CHAPTER VI.

CAPTAIN BIDDULPH'S DEPARTURE FOR MARALBASHI—HIS ACCOUNT OF JOURNEY AND COUNTRY—FOREST—WILD CAMELS—GAZELLE—HAWKING PHEASANTS AND HARES—MARALBASHI TOWN AND FORT—DOLAN PEOPLE—SOLDIER'S STORY—TIGERS—TRAINED HUNTING-EAGLES—ANCIENT CITY—STAGES TO AKSU—RETURN TO KASHGHAR—PRESENTS OF GAME—*OVIS POLI*—BLACK IBEX—GAZELLE—FROZEN DRAWING STUDIES—MARAL—WILD BOAR HUNTING—MR. FORSYTH'S VISIT TO ARTUSH—DR. STOLICZKA AND CAPTAIN TROTTER'S EXPLORATIONS—TURKISH PROTECTORATE OF KASHGHAR—YANGI SHAHR.

MARALBASHI (the stag's haunt), lying away to the east towards Aksu, was visited by Captain Biddulph while we were away in the Tian Shan. Captain Biddulph is the first European traveller in that direction, and the following is his description of the country and journey:—

"The Ameer's permission for my going to Maralbashi having been granted, I left Yengi Shahr, Kashghar, on 31st December, accompanied by Mirza Sufee, a Punjabashi, who had orders to look after me and make all necessary arrangements.

"I reached Maralbashi in seven marches, the distance from Kashghar being about 120 miles. The road runs for the entire distance along the course of the Kizzil Su or Kashghar river, which it crosses about sixty-six miles from Yengi Shahr.

"Passing the villages of Barin, Randomar, Arowah, and Yandomel, we crossed by bridges two considerable streams, the Terbuchek and the Chokanak, flowing from the south into the Kizzil, about three miles apart, and darkness having come on we halted for the night in the village of Sang.

"The Punjabashi knocked at the door of the first house we came to, and demanded quarters for the night. No difficulty was made, though of course we were unexpected guests, and I do not suppose any European had ever been seen in Sang. I was shown into the principal room, where they were preparing for the evening meal before retiring to rest. The family teapot and soup kettle were on the fire, and a quarter of mutton hanging up showed they were well off for eatables. The room was clean and neat, affording a great contrast to a house of like pretensions in an Indian village. The walls were truly made, with neat niches to serve as cupboards, and in front of the fireplace was a wooden block, sunk level with the ground, to chop wood upon. A seat was made for me by the fire, and while the master of the house went off with the Punjabashi to get ready another room, his wife produced melons and invited me to partake, and without any awkwardness or shyness kept her place by the fire, trying to keep up as much conversation as my limited knowledge of Toorkee would permit. My small dog, which sat up and begged, seemed to afford her great amusement, and she pulled a small boy out of bed to look at it.

"Leaving Sang early next morning we marched to Fyzabad, a large market town, which gives its name to the flourishing district around. At two miles from Sang we crossed the Fyzabad stream, flowing from the south into the Kizzil. This and the two streams crossed the previous day are united into one stream, called the Yamanyar, at no great distance from where I crossed them. Farther on we passed the villages of Kazan Kul and Shaptul; a weekly market is held at the latter.

"Beyond Fyzabad habitations became scarcer, and ceased altogether at Yengi Awat, forty-six miles from Kashghar. Beyond

Yengi Awat the country is covered with low bush jungle and sand-hills, gradually changing to forest, which becomes continuous shortly after crossing the Kizzil Su. Between Yengi Awat and Maralbashi the only habitations met with are robats or post-houses, at intervals of about fifteen miles, which are erected for the use of travellers. These are all of inferior construction, with little accommodation, one of them only consisting of a single room. As I took no tents with me, I used the post-houses during the whole time of my absence from Kashghar.

"The forest, though apparently of great extent, contains no fine timber, the only tree being the poplar (tograk) of stunted growth; the undergrowth consists of a bush growing to a height of about eight feet, a thorny bramble, and camel thorn, but there is no grass. The soil is very dry, alluvial, and covered with a thin hard crust of soda, which crackles under foot at every step, and in which horses sink up to their fetlocks. The forest abounds with gazelles (*Antilopa gutturosa*) and hares, but is otherwise singularly wanting in animal life. For a space of about three-quarters of a mile on each side of the river there are no trees, but in their stead a belt of thick high grass, like what is known in Indian jungles as nurkut, growing to a height of from eight to twelve feet. In this are tigers, wolves, the large deer called by the natives "bugha" or "maral," gazelles, foxes, and pheasants. This treeless belt is doubtless caused by periodical changes of the river-bed, of which there are many evidences. The fall of the country to the eastward is little over 500 feet in 100 miles, according to aneroid readings taken daily. The river makes frequent turns and windings, and is level with its banks, so that a very slight flush of water would cause an overflow. The current is not rapid, and the river is frozen so hard in winter that loaded carts cross it without difficulty. It is crossed in summer by a bridge, which, however, I did not see, as I was able to save several miles by taking a short cut and crossing on the ice in another place. It varies from 70 to 100 feet in width.

"At one of the robats I had an interesting conversation with a traveller who was also putting up there for the night. He was an Aksu official, and had lately come from there with a presentation horse for the Ameer, and having delivered it was on his way to Khoten, where his brother was a Cazee. He told me there was a direct road from Aksu to Khoten, lying through jungle the whole way. He had visited Turfan, and said he had himself seen wild camels two marches to the east of it, and spoke of them as not being very wary, but smaller than domestic ones. I questioned him as to the existence of wild horses or asses in the desert eastward, but he said he had never heard of any.

"At Togha Sulook, between 40 and 50 miles from Maralbashi, I stopped for a day's shooting. The only game I got was

THE DJERAN.

one very good specimen of the gazelle, or, as the people there call it, djeran. The buck measures $27\frac{1}{2}$ inches at the shoulder, and greatly resembles the common Indian gazelle, except that the horns are rather longer and curve outwards, the tips being turned sharply inwards towards one another, making a very handsome head.

"The next day on the march I was met by a Yuzbashi, who had been sent out to meet me. He had brought a pair of trained hawks with him, and as we marched we beat along, keeping a few yards off the road, and took several hares with them. The hawks seemed to have no trouble in holding a full-grown one, and the hare was often taken within 30 or 40 yards of where he was put up, even among the brambles and bushes. The trembling of the hares when taken from the hawk was very curious; they seemed quite paralysed with terror, in a way I never saw before in animals of the kind; otherwise they were quite uninjured. Just as we got to our halting-place for the night, one hawk was flown at a cock pheasant, which, after a flight of 150 yards through the high trees, dropped in some thick brushwood; the hawk at once took perch above him, and we put up the pheasant again. In this way we had three flights, the pheasant escaping at last in a large extent of brambles, out of which we could not put him. This was in thick forest, but the men said if both hawks had been flown they would have killed. It was curious to see the hawk each time perching guard over the places where the pheasant had dropped, waiting for us, and watching every movement while we beat. The flight of the pheasant, when once fairly on the wing, though short, is so rapid that the hawk has no chance of striking him, but by perching high above him when down he is generally able to strike him as he rises a second time.

"Within four miles of Maralbashi the forest ceases, and the country is covered with long grass, varied by occasional patches of scrub and swamp, much resembling the Rohilcund Terai. In this are dotted about small villages, with patches of cultivation round them. The grass jungle extends over a great extent of country, as well as I could gather, to the north-east, south-west, and eastward, being doubtless formed by the overflows and changes of course of the Kizzil and Yarkund rivers. The latter, I was informed, flows close to Aksakmaral, about 32 miles south-west of Maralbashi.

"Maralbashi, which is also known as Burchuk and Lai Musjid, contains about 1500 inhabitants, and is at the junction of the road from Yarkund with the Kashghar and Aksu road. It contains a fort and small garrison of about 200 men; it could, however, from its position, be easily and quickly reinforced from Aksu, Kashghar, or Yarkund, if necessary. In the time of the Chinese occupation it was no doubt an important point, as they had internal rather than external troubles to guard against.

"The fort is of the same kind as others we have seen in the country, with earthen rampart about 30 feet thick and 25 feet high, a low parapet forming a kind of covered way, and ditch. It forms a square of about 170 yards, with projecting circular bastions at the angles, three of them having square towers on them: also a circular bastion in the centre of each face.

"The river Kizzil flows under the walls of the fort, and during the late rebellion against the Chinese was made use of by being dammed up and turned on to the fort to break down the rampart. Where I crossed it on the road from Kashghar it is 100 feet wide, level with the bank, but flows here in a greatly diminished stream about 25 feet wide between high banks, 20 feet below the level of the surrounding country. Its character was so altered that it was only after repeated assurances from the people that I satisfied myself as to its being the same stream.

"Close outside the fort is a palace lately built by the Ameer, who often stays here on his way to and from Aksu.

"The natives of the district are called Dolans; they have a more Tartar-like cast of countenance than Yarkundees and Kashgharees, and are said to be distinguished by their fondness for music and singing. They are said to be descended from prisoners brought in the fourth century of the Hejra by Haroun Bugra Khan from Transoxiana, and forcibly settled in the country between Maralbashi and Kuchar. In the jungle villages they excavate houses out of the ground, making grass roofs level with the surface. The term Dolan is, I believe, applied generally to people of mixed parentage.

"The present Hakim Beg of Maralbashi, Ata Bai, has the title of Mirakhor. He is an Andijani, about thirty-five years of age, with especially pleasant address, and seems much liked by the people, who all speak well of him. He was not in Maralbashi when I first arrived, having been away for ten months with the troops at Orumchee and Manass. Four days after my arrival he returned with about 120 men. I was told that during the recent campaign under the Ameer's son, a great number of desertions had occurred in the army; upwards of 400 men, it was said, had deserted into Russian territory. Of the contingent from Maralbashi four had been killed and twenty had deserted.

"In Ata Bai's absence I was received by the deputy governor, Moolla Samsakh, who showed me every attention. The whole of the public robat was placed at my disposal, and all supplies I stood in need of were furnished.

"On one occasion a man forced his way into my room and rather rudely demanded in Persian a turban as a present, similar to one I had given another man the day before. He told me that he was the Moolla Aloyar, and a Cazee, and reiterated his demand for the turban in a very impudent way. I told him that I was not in the habit of giving turbans to people who asked for them, and he went away as abruptly as he had entered. I sent for the Punjabashi, and told him that I did not like people coming into my room without invitation, and would never give anything if I was asked for it. He said it should not happen again, and half-an-hour afterwards I received a message from the Moolla Samsakh, saying that I should not be troubled again, and that the Cazee had been severely beaten for his insolence. I was told afterwards that the punishment had given great satisfaction in the bazaar, where Moolla Aloyar was disliked on account of his constantly asking people for things which they dared not refuse.

"At Maralbashi I found a Punjabee, named Gholam Khadir, serving as a soldier. His son, a sharp lad of thirteen years of age, was sent over to stay in the robat to interpret for my servants. I told him I should like to see his father, who accordingly came over the same evening. I had a long and interesting conversation with him, in which he told me his history as follows:—' Two years ago I left Sealkote with six ponies laden with merchandise to sell at Leh. When I arrived there I found no sale for my goods, so I resolved to come on to Yarkund, being advised to do so by Mr. Shaw. In crossing the Suget pass all my ponies perished, much snow having fallen, and I lost everything. There was only my son, the boy you have seen, with me, and a servant who went mad with the troubles of the journey. Another trader helped me on to Sanju, and from there the Hakim forwarded me on to Yarkund. I was taken before the Dadkhwah, who was very good to me, and gave me two hundred tangas and some clothes, and told me I should go back to the Punjab in the spring. When I again went before him in the spring, he told me I ought to be married, that everybody in the country was married. I protested that I had a wife in Sealkote, but he said that did not matter, and sent for a Moollah, who was ordered to find me a wife, and I was married. When all my money was gone, I went again to the Dadkhwah, who sent me to Kashghar, where I was recognised by Mirza Shadee, who had seen me in Sealkote. I used to make medicines, and give them to people at Sealkote, and gave some to Mirza Shadee when he was there. I once gave some to Ata Bai, the Hakim here, and cured him. He gave me a robe and eight tangas for it. I was taken before the Atálik, who asked me what I could do. I answered that I doctored people, and I was sent off to this place with my son. Guns were put into our hands, and we have been here ever since. Four months after my arrival my wife was sent to me here from Yarkund. My son and I get each a robe once a year, enough to eat, and one hundred tangas between us. All soldiers get about the same, a few get eighty to an hundred tangas yearly. A Punjabashi gets three hundred tangas and two robes, a Yuzbashi three hundred tangas and three robes. Zemindars are never taken to be soldiers, but all men who can give no account of themselves are made to serve in the ranks. The Chinese used to take zemindars for soldiers. Two hundred men went from here with Ata Bai to Orumchee, where there has been much fighting. About 300 Chinese prisoners were sent from there some months ago, and forced to become Mussulmans. Ata Bai is a good man, so is the Yarkund Dadkhwah. There is much petty theft here, but no burglary; robbers are not daring as they are in India. The first time a man is caught stealing he is led all round the bazaar and beaten, the second time he has one ear cut off, the third time his right hand. I have never heard of a man being hanged for stealing. I once saw a man's throat cut in the bazaar, but that was for murder. I have never seen a man hanged. The gallows is put up to frighten people. The punishment of death is only inflicted for murder. I remember two murders while I was in Yarkund. Everybody is married, even all the soldiers: when one dies, his wife is given to another. All marriages are arranged by the Moollahs. When a man wishes to get rid of his wife, he turns her out of his house, and has by the Sharyat to pay her ten tangas, and give her clothes. At the end of three months she may marry again. The women here are very bad, they have no shame. All eatables, except mutton, are very cheap. A great deal of beef and horse flesh is eaten. Taxes on produce are paid in kind to the extent of 4 per cent. People are constantly saying that there used to be much fun and wine-drinking in the time of the Chinese, now there is none. The women especially are continually lamenting this. When people were very poor they used to sell their children to the Chinese for a yamboo (£17). If at the end of a year they could repay the yamboo, the children were returned to them. When you arrived in Yarkund, it was rumoured that 700 or 800 sahibs had come: that you had come in consequence of the visit of the Russian Embassy last year. I was in Kashghar then and saw them. The Ameer is much pleased at your coming. When Mr. Shaw first came he was placed in 'nuzzurbundee' (under surveillance); so was the sahib who came afterwards to Yarkund: now the Ameer knows you better, and you are allowed to go where you like.'

"From Maralbashi I went to Charwagh, a village of about 250 inhabitants, 14 miles on the Aksu road. I was especially anxious to shoot a tiger, of which there were many about, but was unsuccessful in the sea of high grass with which the country is covered. From footprints and skins, and judging by what I was told, there is no doubt that the tiger here is altogether a smaller animal than the Indian one. He seems also to differ considerably in his habits, prowling round villages at night, killing dogs and sheep, and behaving more like an Indian panther than a tiger. The people spoke of men being killed by tigers occasionally, but it does not appear to be a common occurrence.

"I had, however, good sport shooting gazelles and pheasants which abounded, and I also saw the burgoots* or trained eagles kill gazelles and foxes. I was not fortunate enough to see them kill a wolf, though they were twice flown, but the animals on both occasions being in thick bush jungle, and at a great distance, the birds did not sight them. Their owners, however, spoke of it as an ordinary occurrence. When the jungle is not too high, they sight their prey at a great distance, and sweep up to it without any apparent effort, however fast it may be going. Turning suddenly when over its head, they strike it with unerring aim. If a fox they grasp its throat with the powerful talon and seize it round the muzzle with the other, keeping the jaws closed with an iron grasp, so that the animal is

* The bearcoot of Atkinson.

THE TRAINED HUNTING BURGUT, GOLDEN EAGLE, OF EASTERN TURKISTAN

powerless. From the great ease with which an eagle disposes of a full-grown fox, I could see that a wolf would have no better chance. Gazelles are seized in the same way, except those with horns, in which case the eagle first fastens on to the loins of the animal, and watching his opportunity transfers his grasp to the throat, avoiding the horns. The burgoot, however, is not very easy to manage, and requires the whole of one man's care. Its dash and courage are great, but if flown unsuccessfully once or twice, it will often sulk for the rest of the day. When it kills it is always allowed to tear at its game for a little time; the men told me that if prevented doing so while its blood was up, it would very probably attack our horses.

"I was enabled by sextant observations to fix the latitude of Maralbashi at 39° 46′ 25″ N.

"Nine miles to north-east of the Maralbashi is a huge black rock, apparently basaltic, with a treble peak, rising to a height of some 2500 feet above the plain. It is very rugged and quite inaccessible, and forms a conspicuous landmark. It is called 'Pir Shereh Kuddum Moortaza Ali Tagh,' 'the Prophet Ali's footstep.' At its foot on the north side is a Mazar of great sanctity. The Aksu road runs within a mile of it, and travellers on catching sight of the shrine dismount and say a prayer.

"From Charwagh I was asked to come on to Tumchuk, some miles farther on the Aksu road. As nothing had been said about it before leaving Kashghar, I decided not to do so, and had reason to repent my decision. On returning to Kashghar I was told that at Tumchuk are the ruins of a very ancient stone city. It happened that, on one occasion while shooting, I came upon a hewn stone looking like part of an hexagonal pillar, but though I made several inquiries of the men with me, none of them said a word about the ruined city. I also noticed that the jungles contained many signs showing that at one time there had been considerable cultivation.

"The country round Maralbashi is well watered, and the soil rich, and seems only to want population.

"The stages beyond Charwagh on the Aksu road were given me as follows by the Moolla Samsakh, who told me that there was a robat at each stage:—

1. Chadyrkul.
2. Yakakuduk.
3. Zoidu.
4. Chilan.
5. Chulkuduk.

6. Soi Langri.
7. Oikul.
8. Kumbash.
9. Aksu.

"I returned to Kashghar on the 23d January in five marches from Maralbashi. The day before I left I paid a visit to Ata Bai in the fort, and thanked him for all the civility I had experienced, presenting him at the same time with a pair of binoculars and a pound of English powder. He presented me in return with a pony, and the next morning a man overtook me on the march with a trained hawk, also sent me as a present.

"No attempt was made at any time in any way to control or direct my movements. I received whatever supplies I was in need of, and was treated by all officials with the greatest civility."

Besides the daily present of bread, fruit, and sweets, sent from the Atalik's table to mark the steady continuance of the high favour in which we stood, a weekly one, on an extensive scale, was always brought by our noble "Mihmandar" Ihrar Khan Tora, when sent by the Atalik to inquire, in the most formal and complimentary manner, after the health of the envoy and the officers of the Mission. This weekly present used to consist of game, large and small, chests of pears all the way from Kuchar, in the far east, famous for that fruit, bags of frozen butter, loaves of Moscow sugar, and trays of Russian "motto" bon-bons. Of game there were *Ovis poli* and black ibex, the "Jerun" gazelle, the pheasant (Shaw) of the plains, and the snow species of the hills, "chikor" or hill partridge, hares, and many kinds of wild fowl.

The *Ovis poli* was the gem of our collection of new and rare animals. The following is the description of it given by Dr. Stoliczka, the naturalist to the Mission, to accompany a sketch made by me, and sent by the Envoy to the London Zoological Society, from Kashghar, in February 1874.

"OVIS POLI, BLYTH.

"*Male, in winter dress.*—General colour above hoary brown, distinctly rufescent or fawn on the upper hind neck and above the shoulders, darker on the loins, with a dark line extending along the ridge of tail to the tip. Head above and at the sides a greyish-brown, darkest on the hind head, where the central hairs are from 4 to 5 inches long, while between the shoulders somewhat elongated hairs indicate a short mane. Middle of upper neck hoary white, generally tinged with fawn; sides of body and the upper part of the limbs shading from brown to white, the hair becoming more and more tipped with the latter colour. Face, all the lower parts, limbs, tail, and all the hinder parts, extending well above towards the loins, pure white. The hairs on the lower neck are very much lengthened, being from 5 to 6 inches long. Ears hoary brown externally, almost white internally. Pits in front of the eye distinct, of moderate size and depth, and the hair round them generally somewhat darker brown than the rest of the sides of the head. The nose is slightly arched and the muzzle sloping. The hair is strong, wiry, and very thickly set, and at the base intermixed with scanty, very fine fleece; the average length of the hairs on the back is from 2 to 2½ inches. The iris is brown. The horns are subtriangular, touching each other at the base, curving gradually with a long sweep backwards and outwards; and after completing a full circle, the compressed points again curve backwards and outwards; their surface is more or less closely transversely ridged.

"The following are measurements taken from a full-grown male, though not the largest in the Mission collection:—

	Inches.
"Total length from between the horns to tip of tail	62
Length of head	13.25
Tail (including the 1½" long hair at tip)	5·5
Distance between snout and base of ear (the eye lies below this connecting line)	12·75
Distance between base of ear and the eye	3·25
Distance between snout and eye	8·5
Distance from the contact of horns to snout	12
Breadth between the anterior angle of eyes	6
Length of ear in front	4·75
Height of shoulder (the hair being smoothed, beginning from the edge of the middle of the hoof at the side)	44
Girth round the breast	51·5
Length of one horn along the periphery	48
Circumference of one horn at base	15
Distance between the tips	38

"The colour of full-grown females does not differ essentially from that of the males, except that the former have much less white on the middle of the upper neck. The snout is sometimes brown, sometimes almost entirely white, the dark eye-pits becoming then particularly conspicuous. The dark ridge along the tail is also scarcely traceable.

"In size, both sexes of *Ovis poli* appear to be very nearly equal; but the head of the female is less massive, and the horns, as in allied species, are comparatively small: the length of horn of one of the largest females obtained is 14 inches along the periphery, the distance at the tips being 15 inches, and at the base a little more than 1 inch. The horns themselves are much compressed; the upper anterior ridge is wanting on them; they curve gradually backwards and outwards towards the tip, though they do not nearly complete even a semicircle.

"In young males, the horns at first resemble in direction and slight curvature those of the female, but they are always thicker at the base and distinctly triangular.

"The length of the biggest horn of male along the periphery of curve was 56 inches, and the greatest circumference of a horn of a male specimen at the base $18\frac{1}{2}$ inches.

"Mr. Blyth, the original describer of *Ovis poli*, from its horns, was justified in expecting, from their enormous size, a correspondingly large-bodied animal; but, in reality, such does not appear to exist. Although the distance between the tips of the horns seems to be generally about equal to the length of the body, and although the horns are very much larger, but not thicker or equally massive with those of the *Ovis Ammon* of the Himalayas, the body of the latter seems to be comparatively higher. Still it is possible that the *Ovis poli* of the Pamir may stand higher than the specimens described, which were obtained from the Tian Shan range.*

* The Tian Shan wild sheep has since been described as the *Ovis Karelini*, a species somewhat smaller than the true *Ovis poli* which frequents the Pamirs.

"Large flocks of *Ovis poli* were observed on the undulating high plateau to the south of the Chadir-Kul, where grass vegetation is abundant. At the time the officers of the Mission visited this ground, *i.e.* in the beginning of January, it was the rutting season."

The horns of wild animals are deposited at the shrines in Kashghar, similarly as at the temples and other places of mark in the Himmalayahs, and at a shrine in the Artush valley Mr. Forsyth saw a pair of *Ovis poli* horns which measured 61 inches. In the course of this narrative I shall tell of a pair measuring $65\frac{1}{2}$ inches, which I obtained on the Great Pamir, and had the pleasure of adding to the National collections in the British Museum.

The Tian Shan ibex merely differs from the Himmalayan species in being darker in coat,—so dark, however, as to cause us to designate it the "black ibex." It appears to frequent the Tian Shan and Terek ranges. The same ibex are said to be found in the Kuen Luen to the south-east of Yarkand. Those I saw on the Great Pamir were of the light-coloured Himmalayan kind.

The "Jerun" gazelle has been already noticed in Captain Biddulph's account of his Maralbashi journey. We had a tame one at Yarkand, of which I was enabled to make many drawings. The game often reached us at Kashghar in a frozen state, when by half thawing selected specimens, I was able to put them into position to be again frozen, and so fixed as studies for the sketch book.

The "Maral," the stag of the Maralbashi and Eastern Turkistan, appears to the ordinary eye to be the same as the "Hungal" (stag) of Kashmir, and by all accounts it is similar to the Persian stag. * Alish Beg, the governor of Kashghar, presented Mr. Forsyth with a full-grown maral which had been caught when young, and tamed to a certain extent. It stood 14 hands high at the shoulder. Its horns were not of any great size; but of two very fine pairs obtained in the city, I show the best in the sketch, the head being that of our maral. This stag was too riotous to permit of his being brought away with the other animals collected for despatch to India, and was returned to his original owner on our departure from Kashghar. Of two burgut (golden eagles) sent with this collection it was fortunate that one reached alive to confirm our accounts of the bird being trained for sport like the hawk, as my sketches of the hunting scenes in which they figure were sometimes regarded suspiciously, as Atkinson's first description of the sport was.

HEAD OF THE MARAL.

Wild hog of an unusually large size are found in the reed thickets on the banks of the Kashghar river, and the sporting propensities of the people are admirably shown in the spirited way in which they hunt the wild boar there. During the Envoy's tour in the Artush district, in the end of February, the villagers at one place assembled to show this sport. They were mounted on the strong active little horses of the country, and carried clubs bent at the end like hockey-sticks, with which they strike the animal on the head till he is stunned, when the death-blow is generally given with some other weapon. As we in India in hog-hunting ride for "first spear," so do these sportsmen ride for "first club." The trained eagle is used in this sport: it is "flown" at the hog on the first favourable opportunity, and generally succeeds, by its sharp and powerful attack, in bringing it to bay, when the men close in with their clubs. On the occasion alluded to a splendid "tusker" was killed in this manner. But from all I heard I should say that the wild boar of these parts is not equal in fighting spirit to his brother of Bengal.

Mr. Forsyth and the main portion of the Mission officers went out on the 14th of February for a tour in the Artush district, Captain Biddulph and myself remaining in Kashghar. The Envoy, with Dr. Bellew and Captain Chapman, returned on the 26th, leaving Dr. Stoliczka and Captain Trotter to pursue their explorations towards Uch Turfan, which they did most successfully, reaching as far as the Belosti pass. Captain Trotter in his "Notes on Recent Exploration in Central Asia," published in last September number of the *Geographical Magazine*, says of this journey, that it led to the discovery that "that portion of the Tian Shan mountains lying to the north and north-east of Kashghar, marked on our maps as 'the Syrt,' and hitherto represented as a high table-land rising immediately above the plains of Turkistan, in reality consists of a series of parallel mountain ranges, running as a rule from west to east, each range increasing gradually in height from the lowest ridge on the south to the main ridge on the north—each range also decreasing in height as it runs eastward. Between these ranges, and running parallel to them, are extensive level plains, at first very little higher than the plateau of Eastern Turkistan, but also successively rising higher and higher towards the north, while at the same time they slope down towards the east; thus, the Tughamati plain, about 45 miles north of Kashghar, is higher by 2000 feet; while the Jai Tupa plain, about the same distance east of the Tughamati plain (of which in all probability it is the continuation) is only about 1000 feet higher than Kashghar. These large plains have generally much grass and fuel, though but little water. At one of our camps, which was under snow, the Kirghiz who were encamped there told me that it was only in mid-winter they could keep their flocks at that particular place, as the snow then lying on the ground served as a substitute for water, which was not obtainable at any other season of the year."

At the festival of the "Kurban" (the sacrifice) on the 28th of January, the Atalik publicly announced the Sultan's protectorate of Kashghar, and assumed the title of "Amír," conferred on him by that sovereign. The Sultan's name was ordered to be used for the future in the "Khutba" or prayer for the reigning sovereign at all the mosques, and coin was struck bearing the name of "Abdul Aziz Khan," and purporting to be issued from the mint of "the protected State of Kashghar." Gold tillas (value about eleven shillings) of the new coinage were distributed in largesse that day by the Amír to his troops and attendants.

The Yangi-Shuhr or fort residence of the Amír at Kashghar encloses quite a small town, besides accommodating a very large guard and a numerous body of attendants. The daily traffic between it and the city, five miles off, is considerable. Covered carts passed to and fro continually carrying passengers, and there was a regular "stand" of these vehicles near the gate. Some of them were "reserved" for women, who appeared to go about and visit a great deal. The daily traffic and passing of people was an interesting scene, and I used to walk on the roof of the Elchi-khana, and take advantage of the opportunity to sketch whatever appeared remarkable.

HUNTING EAGLE SEIZING A FOX.

CHAPTER VII.

THE ARMY—ARTILLERY—JEMADAR DADKHWAH—INFANTRY—TAIFURCHIS—CHINESE
CORPS AT DRILL—ARMY SYSTEM—KASHGHARIS—FOOD SUPPLY—TRANSPORT—
ANNUAL VISIT OF GOVERNORS TO THE CAPITAL—KHOTEN REVENUE—JADE—
CHINA TEA TRADE—POLITICAL SYSTEM—SEVERITY OF THE LAWS—SHEEP AND
CATTLE STEALING — THE AMÍR'S PERSONAL GOVERNMENT — MISSION LEAVES
KASHGHAR—ARRIVES AT YANGI HISSAR—YAKUB, THE POLISH DESERTER.

WE had opportunities during our stay at Kashghar of seeing the "regular forces" there, which doubtlessly well represented the character and condition of the Amír's army distributed throughout his territory, to Khoten on the south and Turfan on the east. The army is divided into artillery, Taifurchis, and infantry. There is no cavalry in our acceptation of the term; a great proportion of the infantry is mounted, but they dismount to use their arms, and the use of the sword on horseback is not understood or ever practised. On one occasion, during our stay at the capital, a display of "tent-pegging" and turnip slicing, with spear and sabre, by the expert troopers of our guide corps escort showed the Andijanis and Kashgaris how far behind their warlike neighbours they are in that respect.

Artillery is little understood by the Uzbegs, though they have an immense respect for that arm. Hindustanis and Affghans are much sought after as artillerymen, some of those now serving having been in our Indian army, or that of the Maharajah of Kashmir, and made their way to Kashghar as a place that offered many advantages to adventurous spirits, and perhaps, in some instances, a refuge from that steadily pursuing punishment which year after year overtakes the notorious murderers of 1857. The chief artillery officer is Nubbi Buksh, a native of Sealkote in the Punjab and a bookbinder by trade, who was trained as a gunner in the Sikh Durbar force under Sher Sing and Tej Sing. He was at Peshawur with Captain Bowie and the other British officers when the Punjab campaign of 1848-49 took place, and left India shortly afterwards to seek his fortune in Central Asia. He made his way through Kashmir and Ladak to the Yarkand territory, entering it by the Kilian pass, where he was detained for three months by the Chinese, then holding Eastern Turkistan. Eventually he passed on to Khokand, and took service with the chief of that khanate.

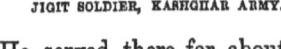
JIGIT SOLDIER, KASHGHAR ARMY.

He served there for about ten years, and was present in the action with the Russians when his master, Alum Kul, the regent, was mortally wounded. While in Khokand he became acquainted with Muhammad Yakub Khan, the present ruler of Kashghar; and after the fall of Tashkend in 1865, he made his way over the Terek pass with 4000 men and joined the Atalik's

standard. Nubbi Buksh is held in high esteem by the Amír as a successful commander who has served him faithfully and well. He is known as the "Jemadar Dadkhwah," and has the reputation of being kind to his countrymen, and assisting them when in need. He is the "Affghan of gigantic stature" noticed by the Russian officers composing the mission sent in 1872 to conclude the existing treaty between Russia and Kashghar. The "Jemadar Dadkhwah's" special command consists of a regiment of comparatively well-armed infantry, with field guns dragged by horses harnessed unicorn-fashion, placed between the companies. He drilled all together before us; the movements were made very slowly, and tolerably precisely on the pattern of thirty years ago then followed in the Sikh army. His words of command were apparently intended for English, and every movement was accompanied by vigorous marching bugle music. Two other similar corps are drilled professedly after the Russian and Turkish systems. Nubbi Buksh showed us some fair shell-practice with a 12-pounder howitzer and a 10-inch

JIGIT SOLDIER, KASHGHAR ARMY.

mortar, at a distance of 1000 yards. He seemed glad to see us, and to talk of the English officers he had seen at Peshawur. He had almost forgotten the Hindustani language, and our conversation with him was chiefly carried on in Persian.

The infantry may be divided into two classes, viz. Jigits and Sarbaz, the proportion being about three-fourths of the former to one of the latter. The Jigits may be described as mounted infantry, every man having a horse which carries all his belongings. They are able to make long and rapid marches, and keep up a daily average of thirty miles for a great distance. In action they dismount to fire, their horses being disposed of in rear, but there is little drill or system among them. The Sarbaz have no horses; as a rule they are better armed and drilled; they are, moreover, kept together in regularly-appointed barracks, and thus subjected to superior discipline. The infantry is distributed in small corps numbering from 200 to 500 men, according to the estimation in which the commanders are held. The firearms are of every kind and bore; matchlocks, fitted with a forked rest projecting beyond the muzzle when closed, Kashmir-made guns, old European sporting guns and rifles, and well executed imitations manufactured in the workshops of Kashghar, Aksu, and Yarkand. The flint-lock is never seen either with gun or pistol. Some American "Spencer" repeating rifles were taken by the Amír's envoy from Constantinople in 1873, and these, I imagine, are the "breech-loading weapons" alluded to in a late rumour as forming the armament of a force despatched from Kashghar to aid in repelling the reported Chinese advance from Hami and Barkul. Target-shooting is much practised. Every town where there is a garrison has a number of musketry butts out-

CHINESE TAIFURCHIS - KASHGHAR ARMY.

side the gates; and during the whole time of our stay at Kashghar, target practice was going on four times a week; it is not, however, conducted on any system, matchlocks, rifles, and double-barrelled guns being all used at the same range together. Lead, sulphur, and saltpetre are very plentiful; the powder made is good, and the dry nature of the climate is favourable to its preserving its quality long.

The Taifurchis are men armed and drilled on Chinese military principles; those in the Amír's service are mostly Chinese and Tunganis. The "Taifu" is a rude sort of wall-piece about six feet long, mounted with a stock; some are used with a matchlock and trigger, others with a priming vent and the old portfire "linstock." It carries a ball varying from one and a half to three ounces, and is managed by four men, two of whom support the stock and muzzle while being fired. They make good practice at 250 yards.

The Chinese Taifurchi corps at Kashghar was paraded for our inspection. About 1200 men were present, divided into companies of ten "taifus" each, accompanied by Andijani standard and colour bearers. There was also a body of spearmen and Kalmak archers with about thirty swordsmen dressed up as tigers, who acted as skirmishers. The "tigers" had large grotesquely painted shields, with short matchlocks fastened across them inside. The movements of each company were directed by fuglemen, and they worked with great precision and rapidity, forming line and column, changing front, firing independently and in volleys, and finally "marching past," the whole being directed by a Chinese commander (the Khu-Dalai) by means of flag signals and beat of drum, forming altogether an interesting sight, and showing an immense aptitude for drill on the part of the men. The "tigers" went through their old Chinese drill of "terrifying appearances" by "tumbling" movements, rolling over and over, advancing firing from behind their shields, and forming themselves into tortoise-like masses to "receive cavalry." The Kalmaks had bows fully five feet long with arrows forty inches in length, thirty of which they carried in quivers slung on the back as shown in the sketch.

The Amír keeps the management of the army entirely in his own hands. The decimal division of command is observed, the ranks being those of commanders of ten, fifty, one hundred, and five hundred, stopping short

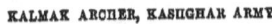

KALMAK ARCHER, KASHGHAR ARMY.

of "Ming-bashi" (head of 1000), though there is "Lashkar-bashi" (head of an army). A great mixture of nationalities is found amongst the soldiers, consisting of natives of the country, Andijanis, Kashmiris, Hindustanis, Affghans, Kunjutis, Wakhis,

Badakhshis, pure Chinese, Tunganis, and Kalmaks. Kirghiz are extensively employed in the frontier militia.

The Kashgharis (by whom I mean the inhabitants of the country extending southeast), though by nature hardy and remarkably able-bodied, are unwarlike, and much averse to military service. The Andijanis, including all the natives of Khokand, are of a warlike spirit, and form the dominant race in Kashghar. Kashmiris (those in the Amír's army are principally Hindu apostates), Hindustanis, and Affghans are much valued as soldiers, and are distributed in small parties among the various corps and garrisons. The Chinese, Tunganis, and Kalmaks, are chiefly prisoners of war, who had their lives spared on consenting to become Muhammadans and serve in the ranks. The pay is small, but is in addition to food and clothing furnished by the State. Desertion is severely punished.

KALMAK ARCHER, KASHGHAR ARMY.

Food is wonderfully plentiful and cheap throughout the

country. At Aksu a sheep sells for two shillings, and at Yarkand for about four and sixpence. The sheep there are heavy and well fed, very unlike the small, spare animals sold at similarly low rates in India. Wheaten flour sells at eighty pounds for two shillings, and Indian corn or maize at forty pounds for sixpence, while large tracts of fertile land lie uncultivated for want of population.

Horses, camels, donkeys, and oxen exist in great numbers. The horses of the country are powerful, hardy, and enduring, averaging fourteen hands in height, and much resembling Welsh ponies in appearance. They carry a load of 250 pounds with ease; the best are bred by the Kalmaks near Karashahr; the average price at Kashghar is £4 : 10s. The camels are of the double-humped species, powerful animals, carrying a 480 pounds load, and capable of standing great extremes of heat and cold. Khoten produces the best and most of these useful animals. The donkeys of the country carry a load of 150 pounds, and are very extensively used in transport between the towns. Carts are also freely used in the traffic of the country; they are generally drawn by four horses, carry 1800 pounds weight, and travel at a rate of three miles an hour on the unmetalled road. Beasts of burden abound to that extent that foot travellers are rarely seen; every one rides on camel or horse, ox or ass.

Indian corn, chopped straw, and dry or green Lucerne grass, according to the season, form the food of all these animals. Lucerne grass grows most luxuriantly, three crops being obtained in one season off the same field, and the same plants produce for three years. Altogether the food supply is so abundant that a starved animal is never seen. While noticing this, also I observed that a corpulent man was never seen. We

ROAD SCENE – KASHGHAR

must suppose that the uncertainties and worries of life under an absolute despotism are against obesity.

About the end of our stay at Kashghar the distant governors began to arrive, according to custom, with the annual imperial revenue and offerings from their provinces, which they always present in person when peace prevails. Hyder Beg, the Hakim of Guma, arrived first, and was followed by Niaz Beg of Khoten, who led in a caravan of 450 camels laden with carpets, silks, cottons, felts, tents, metal dishes, and other local manufactures; two "arabas" (carts) each carrying 1500 jings (equal to about 1800 pounds) of gold and silver; two similar cart-loads of "su-tash" (superior jade); 150 led horses, and 500 donkeys laden with copper coin other than that of Khoten, calculated to represent about Rs. 40,000 or £4000.

The jade is taken by merchants to Kuldja, there to be bartered for tea, and it thence finds its way to China. The rebellion and revolution by which Eastern Turkistan was lost to China caused an entire stoppage of all trade between the two countries, but latterly it has been revived by the Nogai and other Russian merchants trading from Almati as a centre with Kashghar and Kuldja (Ili). Thus jade is now supplied to meet the continued Chinese demand, and Kashghar gets cheap China black tea, which is largely consumed there. Shaw mentions the great increase in the price of China tea at Kashghar during his stay there in 1868-69, from what it was during the Chinese rule; but the price has fallen considerably since, and in the winter of 1873-74 China black tea from Kuldja was selling there at two shillings and twopence per pound. Indian tea was then for the first time introduced to the Kashghar market by a Hindustani trader, but I did not hear with what result. The mass of the people require a cheap article, and now that the China market is made to supply them through Russian means, the Indian traders must be satisfied in the future with less great profit than they have been in the habit of getting. With a shorter and easier route than that now in use, they could yet successfully compete with the Almati merchants, by supplying good Indian black tea instead of the expensive green kind which they at present carry to the Yarkand market.

The Hakim of Khoten was to be followed by the Dadkhwah of Yarkand, whose brother, Ishak Jan, preceded him with a preliminary present of nine (the lucky number) of everything; but the approaching departure of our Mission in the direction of his province caused the visit to be postponed.

I have already alluded to the Amír's Mirzas or secretaries appointed to reside at the local capitals and send direct to him reports of all occurrences and rumours. By means of these and the secret police the Amír keeps himself acquainted with all that is said or done, true or false, and is fully prepared for the discussion of local affairs with the governors, when they appear annually before him. There seems to be no system of accounts : the local administration pays its own expenses, civil and military, and contributes to the imperial treasury. Increase of this contribution is of course understood to carry with it rise in the royal favour, and continuance in power, if it comes unaccompanied by well-founded complaints of oppression or excessive taxation. The political system may be said to be that of ancient Persia, which is almost always followed in the East.

Snow fell twice only, during our winter at Kashghar : once in the end of February, when it hardly covered the ground, and again on the 12th of March, when it lay to the depth of a

THE YANGI SHAHR - KASHGHAR FROM THE ROOF OF THE EMBASSY QUARTERS LOOKING S - THE KIZIL ART MOUNTAINS IN THE DISTANCE.

foot. Up to the latter time the atmosphere had never been quite clear all round: the haze peculiar to Eastern Turkistan always obstructed any complete view of the surrounding mountains. But after the second snowstorm the air was clear, and we had a glorious panoramic view, extending from the Tagharma peak in the south, round by the Kizil Art, Alai and Terck ranges towards the west, to the Tian Shan in the north, and dying away towards Uch Turfan in the far east.

The stern application of severe law, doubtlessly very necessary to put down the violence and disorder which must have grown up in the country after years of internal war, has resulted in a security to life and property probably unequalled for ages past in a purely Eastern state. Crime accordingly is rare. We only heard of one execution during our stay at Kashghar—that of a man for the murder of a boy, whom he killed with the view of removing the evidence against him of the theft of a goat. Ordinary theft is no longer punished with the loss of a hand, but sheep and cattle stealing is still so punished, with the object of giving greater protection to property, the nature of which exposes it to increased risks. I heard of a case of horse-stealing at Kashghar, in which four men were punished with the loss of a hand each, for the theft of a horse; one being the thief, the second and third the buyer and seller, proved to have been aware of the animal being stolen property, and the fourth, a witness convicted of perjury. The last-mentioned came at once to the Mission hospital (having heard of the very skilful surgeon there), carrying his severed hand, and asked to have it put on again! Dr. Bellew was away from Kashghar at the time, and his Hindustani assistant reported the matter to me, and dressed the arm, after which the poor wretch went away taking the hand with him. I have no doubt that he departed believing that had the famous English Hakim (physician) himself been there his hand would have been restored as the other. Dr. Bellew was well known wherever the Mission went for kind and successful treatment of the many medical cases brought to him.

We had our final interview with the Amír on the 16th March, previous to our departure the following day. We were his honoured guests from first to last while within his territory, and were everywhere well received by his people. At one of our previous interviews, on Mr. Forsyth mentioning the good services rendered to us by the Mihmandar Ihrar Khan Tora, and the Dadkhwah of Kashghar, Alish Beg, the Amír said in reply, "Every one is ready to serve my guests, be he Tora or Khoja, Dadkhwah or Mulla" (prince or priest, ruler or scribe). Whatever the severities he practised when striving for power, or the means he took to secure and strengthen his supremacy, it seems certain that now his rule is good, though stern. He is about fifty-five years of age, and in full vigour of mind and body. He exercises a very watchful care over all the affairs of his kingdom, and appears determined to keep and hold, by his individual energy, what he has gained by his own boldness of action, superior ability, and military skill. The fatalist's creed is not his. He does not give himself up to pleasure and indolence, and say, as many Orientals under similar circumstances would, "God gave me the country, and if He wishes me to keep it He will keep it for me." Muhammad Yakub shows by his energetic and vigorous personal government that this is not his way of thinking. He works for beneficial results, and for continuing good from his own labours. With a settled succession and a firm rule such as he has established, the tranquillity of Eastern Turkistan is secure, and its prosperity certain.

The Mission left Kashghar on the 17th March, the envoy being saluted with artillery similarly as on arrival. Synd Yakub Khan Tora accompanied us part of the way. All those who had been about us seemed sorry to see us go; they had all learnt to like us; we never had any trouble with them, and gave them none. The roads were in a very different state from that in which we found them on the way up in December. Now they were deep with mud and melting snow, the effect of the snow-storm of the 12th. Our old friend, Khul Muhammad, the Pansad-bashi in command of the Yangi-Hissar fort, met us some distance off with a repast as before. The Governor received us near the town, and the troops were drawn up outside the fort as we passed to the same quarters which we occupied on the journey up.

Shortly after our arrival at Kashghar when out for an afternoon ride, we were joined by a man, who, entering into conversation, offered to show us shooting in the neighbourhood. We spoke in Persian, but once or twice I thought he used the word "Yes" in reply to questions and remarks. He had light hair and a fair complexion. I began to suspect him to be European, and noticing his poor circumstances, I offered him service in our baggage train, for which a few men were then wanted. He expressed his readiness to take service, and made his appearance the next day to engage in it; but on Mirza Yakub, the official in direct charge of all about the embassy, hearing the matter, he had the man removed, saying that he was a Dah-bashi (commander of ten) in the Amír's service, and could not be allowed to lower himself to menial service. Yakub, for that was this waif's name, showed again one day with a burgut (eagle) for sale, on which occasion I took his likeness. On the day of our departure he was among the crowd at the gateway, and being in want of a man to ride one of the ponies in an ambulance for a sick trooper of the escort, he volunteered to accompany us for the work. He mounted and came away without any further preparation. While I was sketching at Yangi-Hissar on the 20th, he and others came about me, and when I had finished they asked me to show the other drawings in the book. I showed what I had done of Khul Muhammad, to see if any would recognise him. Yakub, looking over my shoulder, read slowly what I had written under the sketch, rendering "the Pansad in command" as "Pansad komadan." I at once turned round, and said to him in English and Persian, "You are English," on which he covered his face with both hands, saying laughingly in Turki, "No, no." He was again removed as before, but knowing that I was to leave for Wakhan the following day he contrived to show himself as I passed the tent of the Yuzbashi, who had taken him in charge, and made a signal of good-bye.

Yakub stated that he was a Nogai Tartar, and spoke of wounds he had received in action, but gave no further account of himself. He lived on charity at a shrine in the neighbourhood of Kashghar, and had a wife and family there. M. Berzenczey, the Hungarian traveller, who reached Kashghar from Almati and Narin after we left, told me at Leh, where we met some months after, that Yakub was a Polish deserter from the Russian service.

CHAPTER VIII.

DEPARTURE FOR SIRIKOL — CHINESE FORT — KIRGHIZ — SEVERE WINTER WEATHER — "STRIKE" OF KASHGHARI ATTENDANTS—KIRGHIZ YUZBASHI—KASKASU PASS— CHIHIL GUMBAZ—TORUT PASS—TANGI TAR—CHICHIKLIK PASS—REACH SIRIKOL VALLEY—TASHKURGAN—EXTENT OF VALLEY—CAPTURE OF SIRIKOL—DEPORTATION AND RETURN OF INHABITANTS — ORIGIN OF THE PEOPLE — OLD TASHKURGAN — CULTIVATION — ANIMALS, DOMESTIC AND WILD — CLIMATE — SOURCE AND NAMES OF RIVER—TAGHDUNGBASH PAMIR AND KIRGHIZ—ROAD TO KUNJUT —SLAVE'S STORY—ATALIK'S FORT—TAGHARMA AND KIZIL ART PLAINS—GREAT AND LITTLE KARAKUL LAKES—MEANING OF "SIRIKOL."

DR. STOLICZKA, Captains Biddulph and Trotter, and myself, left Yangi-Hissar for Sirikol and Wakhan on the 21st March. Including ourselves, our party numbered forty-one, with fifty-eight riding and baggage horses. We were accompanied by Yuzbashi Rustum and five Kashghari soldiers, who, with our own five sepoys of the Punjab Frontier Guide Corps, formed our escort to Wakhan and back. We were preceded by Resaidar Muhammad Afzal Khan, who left the previous day with a letter to Mír Futteh Ali Shah, the ruler of Wakhan, informing him of our proposed visit. Muhammad Afzal reached Kila Panja on the 2d April, and rendered admirable service in making preparations there for our arrival.

Our first day's journey was to Egiz-yar, a large village on the verge of the plain, and the last in the inhabited country towards the hills. The road lay in a south-westerly direction, passing by several flourishing villages amidst extensive cultivation. Six miles beyond Egiz-yar the road enters the hills along the course of a feeder of the Yangi-Hissar river. At this point the passage from Sirikol to the plains is defended by an old Chinese fort situated on the left bank of the stream, with high loopholed walls extending up the hills on both sides of the narrow valley mouth. The plain preserves its even surface right up to the high ranges and ridges which stand out and rise from it, without any undulating or broken ground intervening. The appearance thus presented is strikingly like that of high bold headlands rising from the sea. A small fortified work, three miles farther up the stream, commands a path which there branches off to Kashghar, *viâ* Opal. Small parties of troops are stationed at both of these posts.

Kirghiz compose the population (a very scanty one) between the plains and Sirikol. They live almost entirely by their flocks and herds, only attempting a little scattered cultivation in the lower valleys. They were kind and attentive to us throughout the journey. We always found their felt tents

KIRGHIZ IN WINTER DRESS.

prepared for our accommodation at each halting-place, till within two days of Tashkurgan, when we entered the inhabited part of the Sirikol valley. The Khirgiz tents, having roof openings, admit of fires inside, and were thus infinitely more comfortable than our own in the severe cold then prevailing.

The signs of approaching spring were showing when we left Yangi-Hissar, but we found ourselves back almost in the depth of mid-winter immediately we entered the hills. The streams were nearly all frozen, and snow lay everywhere, while fresh falls were frequent, the whole way to Wakhan and during our stay there. The snowfall in those regions generally takes place in February and March, and it lies till April and May. We started on our journey at almost the most unfavourable time of the year for exploration on the great Pamir highlands, but as it was a matter of no choice, and of the work being done then or probably never by us, advantage was taken of the only opportunity offered. The Turki baggage drivers, whom we engaged at Kashghar for service with our transport train, objected strongly to a return to winter weather, and on the third day "struck" work and refused to proceed. During all our journeys and stay in Eastern Turkistan, we were always treated and known as the Amír's "guests," and an allusion made to the Yuzbashi regarding the inconvenience that would result to the "guests" from these men being allowed to leave, had the effect of bringing about an arrangement by which they were induced to remain. These same men, fourteen days afterwards, on reaching Sarhadd, and finding the weather becoming worse instead of better as expected, left the baggage ponies and declared their determination to return with the Sirikolis, then going back to Tashkurgan; but the Yuzbashi Rustum succeeded in impressing upon the leaders so forcibly the necessity of continuing with our party as long as he did, that we had no further trouble with them. It was very different with the natives of India who accompanied us throughout that trying journey. They bore the intense cold and hard work with remarkable endurance and courage.

We followed the Yangi-Hissar tributary stream by a fair road up to the Kaskasu pass (12,850 feet), which we crossed on the fourth day. Snow and ice made the crossing of it (which is otherwise easy) extremely difficult. Our baggage ponies managed to clamber laboriously up the icy ascent, but the deep fresh snow at the descent necessitated their relief by yaks, which were furnished by the friendly Kirghiz. Our party was joined here by Hyat Muhammad, a Kirghiz Yuzbashi, in military command of the Kirghiz in the Sirikol district, and in direct charge of the roads leading to Yarkand and Yangi-Hissar. He professed to be a true Kirghiz, but from his regular features and full beard, great height and muscular appearance, was very unlike one of that people. He more resembled the Kipchaks, who form the link between the nomad and non-nomad inhabitants of Turkistan. Hayat Muhammad gave much valuable information, which we had afterwards many opportunities of testing and confirming, by inquiring from Sirikolis, Wakhis, and Kirghiz. He accompanied us to Tashkurgan, and again joined us there on the return journey.

For about thirty miles from the plains on the road to Sirikol the hills are bold and precipitous, rising abruptly from the valleys. Poplar and willow trees, and grass, grow by the streams, but the hill-sides are almost wholly devoid of vegetation. Beyond that distance the hills become sloping and rounded, and in summer are covered with excellent pasture, affording extensive grazing for the flocks of the roving Kirghiz.

The descent from the Karkasu pass is to Chihil Gumbaz (forty domes), where we expected from the name to find some interesting ruins. We were also encouraged to expect this from the place being sometimes spoken of as Chihil Situn (forty pillars), and the combined mention of dome and pillar naturally led to the idea of a building more remarkable than any yet seen by us in Eastern Turkistan. We found, however, only one or two small clay-brick domed Kirghiz tombs in a ruined state, and learnt that the name of the place was derived from forty such having at one time existed there. A road branches off from this point to Yarkand, distant 110 miles, passing down the Charling valley and stream, and bearing about due east. In the time of the Chinese occupation this passage was watched by an outpost. The streams from the southern side of the Kaskasu pass and the eastern of the Torut unite here and form the Charling, which flows into the Yarkand river.

The fifth day's journey took us over the Torut pass (13,330 feet), which, with the hills all about, had an almost unbroken covering of deep snow. We saw a great many snow-pheasants on this pass. Willow and poplars are plentiful in the valleys below, and give an abundant supply of firewood. Cultivation on a small scale is carried on at Bas Robat, the halting-place between the Torut and Chichiklik passes. The streams from these unite at Bas Robat, and flow in a south-easterly direction into the Yarkand river.

We proceeded on the sixth day to the foot of a great elevated slope leading to the Chichiklik pass, plain, and lake (14,480 feet). Two or three miles of this day's march lay through the "Tangi Tar" (narrow way), over about the worst bit of road we met with throughout the journey. The Tangi Tar is a very narrow defile, with a stream rushing over boulders and fallen blocks of rock flowing through it, and occupying the roadway to such an extent that in many places its bed is the only available passage. Holes cut in the wall-like sides of the rocky banks, at one particularly confined part, show that in former times the passage was by means of a supported stage- way above the water. The attendant Kirghiz also mentioned this. There are several hot springs in this gorge, temperature about 116°, and there are many at the Yambulak (hot spring) pass in its immediate vicinity. Birch, willow, and gigantic juniper grow plentifully here. As the season advances, the Tangi Tar and Shindi defiles become impassable, by the streams which flow through them to the east and south from the Chi- chiklik slopes swelling from the melting of the snow, and then the road by the higher Yambulak and Kok Moniok passes is fol- lowed. Both of these passes lead down to the Chichiklik plain and small lake, which lie between them in a loop formed by the ranges which they traverse.

The snow lay deep and heavy on the Chichiklik slope, and our horses, stiffened with their hard struggle the previous day over the sharp rocks and through the half-frozen torrent of the Tangi Tar, had a toilsome pull up it, followed by a very troublesome descent through the stony Shindi ravine leading to the Yarkand or Sirikol river, which we reached on the 28th. We here came upon the first Sirikoli village and cultivation. I had no difficulty in conversing with the people, all appearing to have a good knowledge of Persian, which was our medium of communication. From this we travelled twelve miles in a westerly direction up the open banks of the Sirikol river to the western descent from the Kok Moniok pass and the junction of the Tagharma stream, at which point the main river, flowing from the south, makes a sharp bend to the east. The open valley of Sirikol begins here, and extends south for a very considerable distance towards the Kunjut mountain range. We encamped on the 29th in the open valley, at a small military post about four miles from the fort (Tashkurgan), where we were met by some of the Kashghari governor's people, sent to welcome us in his name to Sirikol. We reached Tashkurgan the following day, the 30th, and were well received and hospitably entertained by the governor, Hussun Shah, who came out some distance to meet us. He was accompanied by a mounted guard, remarkably well appointed, and neatly dressed. Hussun Shah himself we remarked to be almost the best dressed and equipped officer we had seen in the Atalik's service. He has the title of Toksabai (Chief of the Standard). We estimated Tashkurgan to be 124 miles by road from Yangi-Hissar, in a general south-easterly direction.

The Sirikol valley is 10,250 feet above the sea. It extends eight miles north of Tashkurgan, to the bend of the river east, and appears to stretch far away south. The average breadth is about three miles. Cultivation is confined chiefly to the western slopes, and is the work entirely of its Tajik inhabitants, who occupy a length of about 15 miles of the valley above and below the fort. The level part, through which the river flows, is used as a pasture ground, and affords rich and abundant grazing. The houses are built of stone and mud, and are all collected in villages and hamlets, none being scattered over the cultivated land as in Kashghar and Yarkand. Most of the villages we

SIRIKOL VALLEY—LOOKING SOUTH.

saw were in a miserable state, the houses having fallen greatly to ruin after the late total deportation of the inhabitants to Kashghar.

During the Chinese occupation of Eastern Turkistan, Sirikol was ruled by a hereditary chief of its own, who, however, professed allegiance to that power. A visit was made to Yarkand every second or third year, to pay a nominal tribute and receive valuable presents, including gold and silver. The money thus given represented a yearly payment of fourteen "yambus" (a little over £200), which was regarded as a subsidy for the military protection of the frontier and the road towards Badakhshan.

The Atalik, in the early years of his rule, had too much in the way of more important conquest to occupy him in the east, to permit of attention being paid to minor matters in the west, and Sirikol, under its chief Alif Beg, escaped notice till 1868. Alif Beg succeeded his father Babash Beg in 1865. The eldest son,

Abul-Assam, having some defect of speech and weakness of intellect, was set aside in the succession in favour of the second, Alif Beg. The Atalik, in ignorance of this, summoned the eldest son to make his submission and acknowledge fealty. Abul-Assam obeyed the command, and presented himself before the Atalik at Turfan. On the mistake being discovered, Alif Beg was summoned without the elder brother being permitted to return. The detention of his brother so alarmed Alif Beg, that he ignored the order and remained in Sirikol, fearing to trust himself in the hands of the then dreaded Atalik. In the end of 1868 troops were sent to enforce the neglected summons, and Alif Beg, on their approach, fled to Wakhan without attempting resistance. Abul-Assam was given rank and employment in the Atalik's army, and also a residence at Aksu, where he now lives. Alif Beg found an asylum with Futteh Ali Shah, the Mír of Wakhan, a hill chief of characteristic independence and generosity, who, to use his own words to me, considered it "shameful to refuse bread and shelter to the unfortunate who are driven into exile by cruel fate."

The Sirikol people were said to be greatly attached to Alif Beg, and the Atalik, fearing insurrection from this cause, if not from hatred of the change to a Suni rule, they being Shiahs, deported the whole population to Kashghar in 1870. They were sent back to their native country after two years' exile. There are now about 600 families of them in the valley and the neighbouring Tagharma plain, representing about 2500 or 3000 souls. They appear contented with the Kashghar rule, and appreciate thoroughly the peace and security they enjoy under it, and their immunity from the terrible "alaman" (raids) of the Kunjutis, Kirghiz, and Shignis, to which they were formerly much exposed. Notwithstanding fellowship of creed, the Kunjutis and Shignis appear to have had no scruples in carrying off and selling into slavery their Shiah brethren of Sirikol.

The Sirikolis are Shiah Muhammadans. They say that they have been in the valley for seven generations as a distinct people, under a chief of their own, and are the descendants of wanderers who came from all quarters—from Badakhshan, Wakhan, Shighnan, Hindustan, Kungut, and Turkistan. Hence, as my informant, Dada Ali Shah, a Sirikol Mulla, said, "The language peculiar to us is a mixture of what is spoken in all these countries." Persian, however, is also spoken by them in common with the inhabitants of the other Shiah states adjacent to the head waters of the Oxus.* They differ in appearance from the Kirghiz, Uzbegs, and inhabitants of Eastern Turkistan, in having regular features and full beards. Their salutation of respect is made with the hand to the forehead, and not with the arms crossed in front as among the Turks. On inquiring for books or MSS., I was told that all had been lost long ago, carried off or destroyed in the repeated slave-hunting raids from which they had suffered cruelly for many years. The Mulla said that he had been plundered of all his books in these dreadful "alamans," of which he had witnessed no less than twenty, but that now they were quite unknown since the establishment of the Atalik's strong rule.

The ancient name of Tashkurgan is Varshidi. The ruins show it to have been of square or rectangular form, with pro-

---

* The idea that they were a remnant of the Uigurs, the original inhabitants of Eastern Turkistan, must give way, I think, to the opinion that they are of Persian lineage, similar to the alien populations of the other small principalities in their neighbourhood, and like them spring from the west.

jecting towers, and built of rough unhewn stone. It does not appear to have been of great antiquity, or very remarkable in any way. The lay Jesuit, Benedict Goës, who passed through Sirikol in 1602-3 on his way from Wakhan to Yarkand, was the first and only European traveller before us who had visited this place. Several accounts from other sources of information had described the fort as a building of hewn stone, and of very ancient date, going back even to the time of the legendary conqueror Afrasiab. The Mulla I have mentioned did not know of it as older than their own history as a distinct people. The construction of its walls appeared similar to that of the old stone towers still standing in most of the villages, which were built for refuge and defence in the man-stealing times to which I have already referred.

The cultivation consists mainly of barley (huskless), beans, peas, carrots, and turnips. The domestic animals are camels, yaks, ponies, oxen, sheep, and goats. The yaks are smaller than the Tibetan species: they are used in the plough for agricultural purposes, but, objecting most obstinately to be driven, they can only be utilised by being led. A murrain carried off nearly all the oxen and cows a year ago, and fresh cattle were being obtained from the lower hills. Of wild animals there are the *Ovis poli* and the ibex, and wild fowl of several kinds. For clothing the universal sheepskin is used with a rough woollen cloth, spun and made up into cloaks and lower garments, similar to what are seen in Wakhon and the countries beyond. Sheepskin stockings with stout leather soles, a cotton or woollen girdle, and sheepskin cap, with a scanty cotton turban when obtainable, complete the ordinary dress of the people. Coarse cotton garments are worn at times by those who can afford the luxury, the material being obtained from Yarkand and its villages. For roofing and other purposes, poplar is the only timber procurable, and it is grown in sheltered spots near the villages. Stunted willow is abundant near the numerous watercourses in the valley flats. The climate is severe. Hussun Shah, the present governor, who has had five years' experience of it, says that there only two seasons, summer and winter, the former lasting three months, the latter nine.

The Sirikol river rises in the Taghdungbash Pamir and Kunjut range at a probable distance of eighty miles from Tashkurgan. It is variously called Taghdungbash, from that Pamir; Tashkurgan, from the fort; Sirikol, from the valley; Tisnaf, from a large village of the name at the foot of the valley; and Yarkand, from the local belief that it is the main head stream of that river. It was of considerable size when we first crossed it, March 29th; the perfect clearness of its waters, the steadiness of its flow (equality of volume day and night), and the severity of the cold, then showed it to be at the usual low winter ebb. It flows east after leaving the valley, and is said to be joined about fifty miles lower down by the Tong, a stream as large as itself, and also flowing from the Kunjut range. A road to Kargalik, with a branch to Yarkand, passes down the river. When we returned from Wakhan, we tried to arrange to proceed by it, but were told that the "Tong" pass, over a mountain of that name, necessarily crossed on the way, was not practicable till the "apricots were ripe," meaning a month later. Alif Beg, the ex-ruler of Sirikol, told me of the difficult nature of this road till the heavy snow of the "Tong" mountain clears off in summer. The Sirikol valley, after extending south for some considerable distance, bends towards the west, and merges in the Taghdungbash Pamir, which appears to be merely a continuation of the valley at a higher elevation. This Pamir lies to the north of and nearly parallel to the Little Pamir, from which it is separated by a broad chain of hills joining with the Neza Tash mountains west of Sirikol, and forming one unbroken range. Kirghiz occupy it for pasture as far as the Kashghar boundary, said to be twenty "tash" (about eighty miles) beyond the fort. The Taghdungbash Kirghiz were originally subject to Kunjut, but some seven or eight years ago, on being attacked and plundered by the Hunza people, they moved bodily to the Sirikol district and settled in Tagharma. On Sirikol falling under the Kashghar rule, the Taghdungbash Pamir was annexed, and its old nomad inhabitants now pasture their flocks there in perfect security. A daughter of Ghazan Khan, the present chief of Hunza Kunjut, is one of the many wives of the Atalik, and this connection, added to the wholesome dread in which the Amír is held, has had a good effect in restraining to some extent the plundering and slave-stealing propensities of the cruel Kunjutis. Mir Futteh Ali Shah, of Wakhan, brother-in-law to the Hunza chief, also took credit to himself for this improved state of things. He told me that, at the Atalik's request, he used his influence with Ghazan Khan, and induced him to order the discontinuance of robbery by his people in Kashghar territory and on the Yarkand and Tibet road.

The road between Sirikol and Hunza lies along the Taghdungbash Pamir to the descent on the southern side of the Muztagh range, and the distance is said to be a little over 100 miles. The Taghdungbash Pamir slopes appear to lead gradually up to the mountain crest, judging from the account given to me by Rusulla, a native of Jummu, and formerly a soldier in the service of the Maharaja of Kashmir, who was taken prisoner in Kunjut and sold into slavery. I give the story of his capture and liberation in his own words:—"Nine or ten years ago I was one of about eighty of the Kashmir troops garrisoning the fort of Chabrot, in Hunza, Kunjut. There were numbers of Kunjutis in the fort also, and they in concert with others outside attacked us when unprepared for resistance, and made us prisoners. About four (three Hindus and one Musulman) were killed in the struggle. We were distributed among our captors and sold as slaves. I was given to a Taghdungbash Kirghiz, and remained with him in Taghdungbash and Sirikol for three years, after which he exchanged me with an Alai Kirghiz for a camel. I travelled with my new master to the Alai, by Tagharma and the Kizil Art, and was there employed in tending cattle and sheep. On becoming old and feeble, six years after, the Mír of the Alai Kirghiz, Timor, son of Ashnadir, gave me my liberty and sent me to Kashghar with some of his people. We went to the house of Abdul Rabman, to whom Timor is related. He asked me to what country I belonged. I said Hindustan, on which he told me of the English being in Kashghar and Hindustanis with them. I went to them and got employment." Rusulla was afterwards sent to Aktagh, on the road between Yarkand and Karakoram, in charge of provisions placed there for use on the return journey, and on our party passing he accompanied the camp to Kashmir. The information he gave regarding the Taghdungbash Pamir corroborates that previously obtained by Mr. Shaw.

The present fort held by the Atalik's troops is a stone and mud structure built on a commanding position among the ruins of the ancient Varshidi (Tashkurgan). It forms the residence of the governor of the district, Hussun Shah, an energetic, resolute-looking man, said to be a native of Karategin. He showed extreme jealousy of our entering his fort, and indicated in the plainest but most courteous manner his desire not to see any of us inside it. When he met us, on arrival, he conducted us with all ceremony to the camp of "akois" (felt tents), which he had prepared for us, a short distance beyond the fort, taking care, however, to lead us by a circuitous route, so as to avoid passing close under its walls. On his leaving, I expressed our wish to pay him a visit of respect that day, and asked what time would be most convenient, but he begged us not to take the trouble, saying that we as the guests were to be visited by him. I regarded this as a mere conventionality of speech, and sent up our attendant Yuzbashi in the afternoon, to say that if agreeable, we proposed to visit him then. This at once brought him down to our camp to pay us a visit. We halted there two days, and the day before departure I again sent the Yuzbashi to offer a visit from us, but with the same result as before; he came to see us, and said he was ashamed to receive us in such a poor apartment as the best in the fort was, and begged us not to think of going, adding that we had already done him great honour in intimating our intention to visit him. This, with the objection that had been made to any of our servants entering the fort, induced us to give up all attempt to obtain any view of the old ruins at a closer distance than a few hundred yards. We passed by the old walls on our way to Wakhan, and saw sufficient to enable us to form the opinion regarding it already given.

The Tagharma plain lies about three miles to the north-east of the Sirikol valley, and is of the same elevation. It is a fine open crescent-shaped flat, about twelve miles long by seven broad, extending from the south-west to the north-east, and is well watered by a stream which flows through it from the north-eastern end, and falls into the Sirikol river. There is an abundance of rich grass in it, and willows grow thickly by the streams. The numerous hot springs in many parts of the plain caused the vegetation in their close vicinity to be considerably in advance of the season. Besides its Sirikoli Shiah inhabitants, who cultivate and reside in villages on the slopes, 100 Taiyat Kirghiz families, under their chief, Krumchi Bi, pasture their flocks and herds on the plain. This plain is separated from that of the Kizil Art on the north by a low rounded ridge, formed by projecting spurs from the opposite mountain ranges—the Neza Tash to the west, and the Tagharma to the east. The ridge forms the watershed between the two plains, the drainage to the north passing into the Little Karakul lake, said to be about twenty miles distant thence, and that to the south into the Tagharma stream. The Bardish pass leads from the watershed over the Neza Tash range into the Aktash valley, which runs almost parallel to the Kizil Art. The Bardish pass leads out nearly opposite the eastern end of the Great Pamir, and about forty miles above Ak-Balik, the point of junction of the Great Karakul lake stream and the Aksu.

According to the accounts given by the Kirghiz, and corroborated by Wakhis and others acquainted with the country, the Kizil Art plain extends in a northerly direction from the Tagharma to the Alai for about 130 miles. It is separated from the Alai by a mountain range, the pass over which is easy. The Kizil Art is of about the same elevation as the Tagharma, and is similar in character to it, being well

THE MUZTAGH (TACHARMA PEAK) FROM TASHKURGAN, SIRIKOL, LOOKING N.

watered and abounding with grass and bush fuel. It is bordered on the east by the mountain range extending and sweeping round from the direction of the Khokand Terek pass and the Alai, and on the west by the Neza Tash. The Little Karakul lake lies in the lower and the Great Karakul in the upper end of this plain. The former gives exit to the Gez or Yamanyar stream, which flows eastward through the Gez defile under the lofty Muztagh (the Tagharma peak) into the Kashghar plain, and there joins some of the numerous branches or canals of the Kashghar river. This lake is said to be about fifteen or twenty miles in circumference, and very deep. The Great Karakul is stated to be between forty and fifty miles in circumference. It receives feeders from the Alai dividing range, and gives rise to the Murghab, which finds its way westward, and flows through Shighnan and Roshan into the Oxus. The Kizil Art is permanently occupied by 1000 Kipchak and Kirghiz families, who emigrated from Khokand seven years ago, under their present chief, Abdul Rahman.

We halted for two days at Tashkurgan, to make arrangements for our journey onwards to Wakhan. The winter was unusually late and severe, and we were warned to expect considerable difficulty on the way over the Little Pamir from deep snow and intensely cold winds. The weather was bright and clear during our stay in the Sirikol valley, and we had a glorious view from our camp of the majestic Tagharma peak (known there as the Muztagh, "mountain of ice"), about forty miles to the north, towering to a height of 25,500 feet, as estimated by Captain Trotter. It looked a perfect mass of snow and ice, and glistened with numerous glaciers.

The meaning of the name "Sirikol" has been made a subject

of discussion and difference among writers and geographers. Latterly it has been generally accepted as signifying the "yellow valley," from the Turki "sarik," yellow, and "kol," valley. Hussun Shah explained to me that he considered the name to be a corruption of the Persian "Sir-i-koh," from the place being at a great elevation. On finding the valley to be a continuation of the Taghdungbash Pamir, I looked upon the governor's explanation as very probable, from the fact of "Sir-i-koh" being the Persian literal translation of the Turki Taghdungbash, both meaning "head of the mountain." Nothing seems more likely than that the Persian-speaking Sirikolis should, on settling in the valley, give it a Persian name, literally interpreting its Turki one.

KIRGHIZ AK-OI (WHITE HOUSE).

LITTLE PAMIR LAKE, EASTERN END.

CHAPTER IX.

ROOF OF THE WORLD—PREVIOUS KNOWLEDGE OF PAMIR TOPOGRAPHY—DEPARTURE FOR WAKHAN—NEZA TASH—RICH GRASS—AKTASH VALLEY—LITTLE PAMIR: ITS LAKE AND STREAM—WATERSHED—SARHADD STREAM—EXTENT OF LITTLE PAMIR —REACH SARHADD—MET BY THE "MIRZADA"—IBEX-HOUNDS—REACH KILA PANJA ON THE OXUS—WELCOMED BY THE MIR: VISIT HIM IN HIS FORT—PRESENT STATE OF PEACE AND SECURITY—TRIBUTE PAID TO KABUL—POPULATION—CONDITION OF THE PEOPLE—ANIMALS—CROPS—THROUGH TRADE—STATE DEBT PAID OFF.

WE were now about to cross the famous "Bam-i-dunya," "The Roof of the World," under which name the elevated region of the hitherto comparatively unknown Pamir tracts had long appeared in our maps. The first noteworthy travellers across the Pamirs were the Chinese pilgrims, Hwui Seng and Sun Yun, who passed in A.D. 518, and were followed in 644 by the more famous Hwen Tsang. Then came that grand old traveller Marco Polo, in 1272, and Benedict Goës in 1602. The accounts, however, given by these were too vague and general to convey any correct idea of the true nature of the country. Wood, in 1838, was the first European traveller of modern times to visit the Great Pamir, and to trace the Oxus to one of its chief sources there. His accurate and full description of the route from Kila Panja to the western end of the Great Pamir lake, as we found on passing over the same ground, left little to be desired or done. Colonel Montgomery's native explorer, the "Mirza," crossed from Wakhan by the Little Pamir, and was the first to "tie together the basins of the Oxus and Tarim by a chain of route measurements and compass bearings with several determinations of latitude." Faiz Buksh, in 1870, crossed by the Great Pamir to Sirikol and Yarkand, and furnished a very detailed and useful itinerary of the journey. There remained, however, several important doubtful points to be cleared up before the topography of the Pamir lands could be understood. The only available descriptions of the Great Pamir eastward of the lake were so meagre and misleading as still to encourage the idea of a far-extending "steppe" from Wood's lake to the Alai. The flow of the Aksu northward from the eastern end of the Little Pamir was considered improbable, by reason of the belief in the existence of this high plain at a greater elevation than the Little Pamir, and the report of a careful observer like the "Mirza" as to the continued flow eastward of the Little Pamir stream, went far to confirm this impression. The geographical information, however, collected by the late Mr. Hayward, and furnished by Muhammad Amin and Faiz Buksh, indicated an indentation in this supposed plain, along which from Aktash a stream flowed north-west "towards Darwaz." Colonel Yule showed in his introductory essay to Wood's *Oxus* that the question of the flow of this stream was a very important one for the adjustment of Pamir topography.

The other doubtful points were the supposed double exit from the Pamir lakes and the Kizil Art Karakul, and the general character and height of the so-called Pamir steppe. The information we obtained from Kirghiz on the Tagharma plain, Wakhi guides (several of whom spoke to having taken part in former years in raids as far as the Alai), and others, determines, I think, the question of the direction of discharge from both Karakul lakes. Colonel Yule, in his essay, says on this point that most of the evidence up to that time tended to the Karakul discharging towards the west, and Mr. Shaw was the first to throw some light on the story of its double discharge, east and west, by telling of the eastern flow from the Little Karakul.

We left Tashkurgan on the 2d of April, escorted by Hussun Shah, who accompanied us to the mouth of the Shindan defile leading out of the valley to the west, on the Badakhshan road. The Governor rode a very fine Turkoman horse, fitted with gold mounted trappings. This was the first and only horse of that breed which we saw in Turkistan. It was a grey, of light muscular body, thin neck, spare head, and firm flat legs of iron-like strength. Our first day's journey was to the foot of the Neza Tash pass, sixteen miles in a south-westerly direction up the Shindan stream, which flows through the defile of the same name and falls into the Sirikol river. The defile at several places is extremely narrow, and shut in closely by precipitous rocks and bold steep hills which rise high above it. The fallen stones and stream boulders make the road particularly bad for many miles. Willow and thorn bushes grow plentifully at the head of the defile, and the hills there lose their bold character, and become rounded and sloping. Our camp was in snow, but large patches of grass free from it were found in the vicinity sufficient for our horses, which ate it greedily, preferring it greatly to the chopped straw we carried for mixing with their grain. This grass was similar to what we found in many parts of the Pamirs, and in the Aktash valley, rich and sweet to the smell, resembling English meadow hay, and relished immensely by our animals. Judging from what we saw of it in the end of winter, it is easy to believe in its fattening properties in summer, as related by Marco Polo and other travellers, and also told us by the Wakhis. Neza Tash, meaning spear-stone, is named from a spear-like pointed rock near the place.

On the second day we crossed the Neza Tash pass (14,920 feet), leading over a high range running about north-west, and encamped at the mouth of the ravine leading down from it to the Aktash valley, travelling a distance of seventeen miles in a general westerly direction. Snow fell in the night time, and our journey for this and the following three days, covering a total distance of seventy-eight miles, was made mainly through snow. We found plenty of grass in scattered patches and brushwood fuel at this day's camping place. We were here joined by a party of Sirikolis with yaks and ponies carrying supplies sent by Hussun Shah to accompany us to Wakhan. Nothing could exceed the Amír's hospitality and kindness to us throughout our long and difficult journey. We and our whole establishment were abundantly supplied with provisions; and on arrival at each day's halting place, even on the wild and desolate Pamir lands, notwithstanding snow and long travel, we were always welcomed with a repast of some sort, prepared by people sent ahead for the purpose. Orders were given for a strong escort, if desired to accompany us from Tashkurgan, but we considered ourselves safe enough with the small party we started with from

AHTASH VALLEY – LOOKING N.W.

Yangi-Hissar, and passed on without adding to our numbers. I afterwards learnt that Rustum, our attendant Yuzbashi, was well provided with gold, and directed to use it in the purchase of supplies in Wakhan should necessity arise.

On the third day we proceeded south up the Aktash valley to its head, where it merges into the Little Pamir, extending east and west, the appearance being that of the same valley making a sharp turn from south to east. The Aktash (white stone) valley takes its name from a high light-coloured rock near its head on the east, and the stream which flows through it towards the north is called Ak-su (the White Water). We followed up this stream into and through the Little Pamir, and traced its rise to the Gaz or Oi Kul (Goose Lake), in that Pamir. This is the stream that I previously mentioned as an important one in determining the flow of Pamir drainage to the east. Colonel Montgomery's famous explorer, the "Mirza" whom I have alluded to in connection with the Aksu, probably lost the stream in the deep snow which lay at the foot of the little Pamir and the head of the Aktash valley, when he passed in February 1869, and the low appearance of the hills at that point led him most likely to believe that the stream he had followed so far there made its way through the Neza Tash range and joined the Sirikol river. It must be borne in mind that the Mirza worked under great difficulties, and had to make inquiries and take observations secretly, so as to avoid, as much as possible, the suspicion with which he was regarded. On the whole, we proved his information to be extremely accurate.

We reached the Little Pamir lake on the fourth day from Tashkurgan, marching forty-five miles on that and the previous day, in a general westerly direction from the Aktash valley.

The thermometer only marked 5° below zero, but we suffered more severely from the cold than we did on the Tian Shan in January, with fifty-eight degrees of frost. Then the air was still in the valleys, but here we were exposed to a strong steady wind from the west, which accordingly blew against us and could not be avoided when travelling. That, added to the sun-glare off the snow—for we had bright weather till the 9th—cut our faces and inflamed our eyes in a very painful manner. On the first of these two days our difficulties were greatly increased by the track being lost in the extensive snow-beds at the head of the Aktash valley, by which our progress was much delayed.

The Aktash valley at about six miles from its head is 12,600 feet above the sea. It runs in a northerly direction from the Little Pamir, across the eastern openings of the Great and Alichor Pamirs, and sweeps into the Siriz Pamir at Ak-balik, the junction of the Aksu with the Great Karakul Lake stream, the Murghab. Its length is said to be about sixty miles, and its average breadth, judging from the twenty miles extent of it over which we passed, is about three miles. It is thickly covered with grass, and is a pasture resort of the Kizil Art Kirghiz. Willow grows abundantly in it and the adjacent ravines where streams run. We left our last firewood at the mouth of the ravine leading from the Neza Tash pass into the Aktash valley. Up to that we had willow and myricaria, but from that on to Langar, west of the Little Pamir Lake, a distance of seventy-eight miles, nothing but a small prickly shrub six or eight inches high, resembling the lavender plant, is to be got for cooking purposes. No wood of any kind grows upon the Pamirs, but this wild lavender plant is found in abundance all over them, and by reason of its woody roots forms a good substitute for

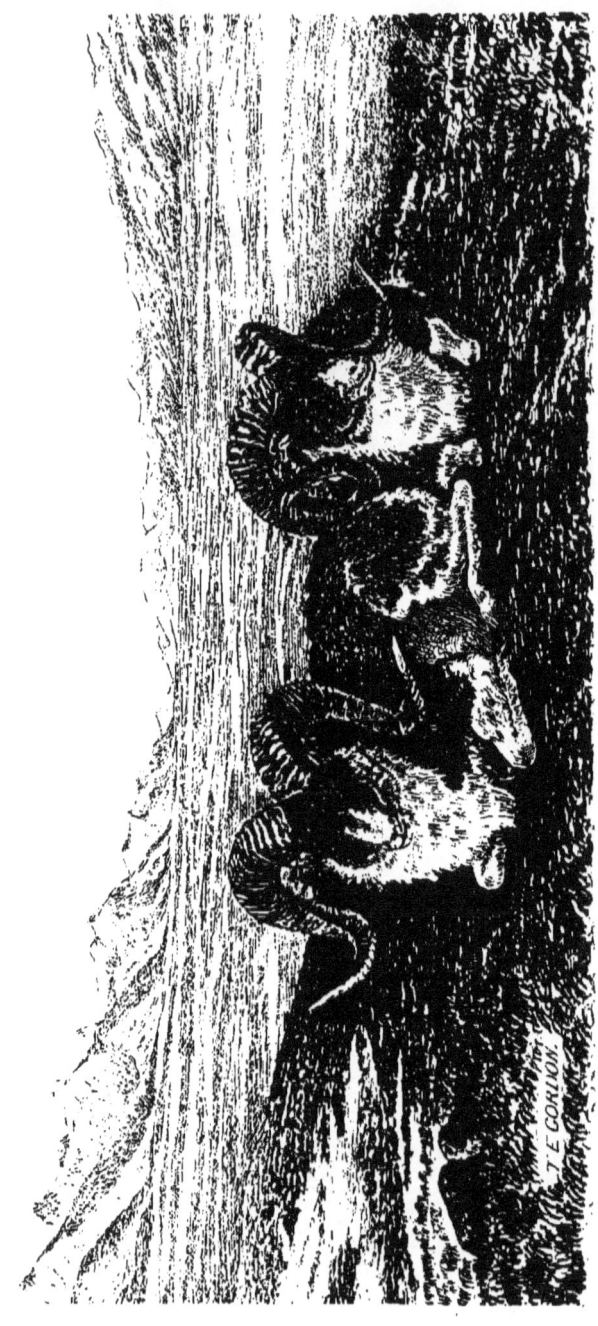

THE LITTLE PAMIR NEAR CHAKMAKTIN OW—WILD SHEEP IN THE FOREGROUND.

bush fuel. It is the same plant which grows all over the highlands of Tibet, and furnishes the only bush fuel obtainable there.

LITTLE PAMIR LAKE, WESTERN END.

The Little Pamir is similar in character to the Aktash valley, and of about the same breadth. It has the same grassy downs, slopes, and flats. It is bounded on the south by the continuation of the Neza Tash range which separates it from the Taghdungbash Pamir. That range appears to sink considerably in height when it turns to the west from the Aktash valley. A broad chain of rounded hills extends on the north of the Little Pamir, and separates it from the Great Pamir. These hills are low towards the Aktash valley, and rise gradually as they approach the lake. The lake is three miles long, and a little under a mile broad. It is broad and deep at the western, and narrow and shallow at the eastern end. We found it and the stream from it frozen. I judged of the relative depth of the opposite ends by observing the surface of the ice towards the east to be undulating, while at the west it was perfectly level. The height of the lake is 13,100 feet. The hills on both sides rise about 2000 feet higher, and those to the south were covered with deep snow. Extensive glaciers and snow-beds lie near the western end. The name "Barkat Yasin" applied to the lake by some native travellers is properly that of a rocky ravine to the north at it's head called "Burgut-Yursi," the "eagle's place or nest." The "r" in "Yursi" is dropped in the pronunciation, as is common in many Turki words, and this probably led to "Yasin" being recorded. Looking due east from the lake, a very fine peak, apparently about 22,000 feet high, showing the glistening of a great glacier near its summit, was very prominent in the range in the far distance.

Our farther journey lay west past the lake. At less than half-a-mile from its head a watercourse choked up with ice and snow appeared, leading west down the valley. Between the lake and this point the rise is very small indeed, and it might almost be supposed that the accumulated debris from the avalanches, and melting snow torrents of succeeding years, had at last banked up a barrier at the narrow valley head there, and driven the lake outlet to the east, where the shores are low and the valley is unconfined. Six miles west of the lake we came upon the ruins of Kirghiz mud and stone huts, and a burial-ground. A stream from the eastern Taghdungbash Pamir joins here. A road leads up this stream to Kunjut over the Khijrui pass. The valley closes in at a distance of ten miles below the lake, and the Little Pamir towards the west may be said to terminate there. This gives that Pamir a length of fifty-eight miles east and west, estimated from the southern extremity of the Aktash valley. The stream (the Little Pamir affluent of the

Oxus, known afterwards as the Sarhadd stream) then runs in a deep set course between high banks rising up to the long mountain slopes, along which, by the right bank, the road leads to Langar, twenty-five miles from the lake. A deserted village and traces of cultivation were observed here, and numerous yaks and cattle were seen grazing on the opposite side of the valley. A stream of considerable size also joins at Langar, flowing from the south-east, and a road goes by it to Kunjut, over the Kura pass.

From Langar the road continues in a general westerly direction along the banks of the stream to Sarhadd. In the depth of winter the frozen surface of the river makes passage up and down easy. We found the ice beginning to break up here and there, and our path had to be sought across and back over the rocky bed, and up and down the high steep banks, making the journey tedious and severe to a degree. In summer the swelling of the stream makes this road extremely difficult, and it is then that the Great Pamir route is followed in preference. Twenty-five miles below the lake, birch, willow, and gigantic juniper appear in thick clumps, and firewood is plentiful from that the whole way to Wakhan and Badakhshan. The valley opens out a mile above Sarhadd, and remains more or less wide to Kila Panja and beyond. Habitation and cultivation commence at Sarhadd and continue down the valley, with large tracts of dense thorn and willow jungle and pasture flats intervening between the villages.

A letter of welcome from Futteh Ali Shah, the Mír of Wakhan, was received at Langar, and we were met at Sarhadd by his eldest son, the "Mirzada" Ali Murdan Shah, who was sent to escort us to his father's fort residence at Kila Panja on the Oxus. The son is a young man of about twenty-five years of age, with fair hair and blue eyes, and pleasing manners. Like all the Wakhis he is very fond of field sports, and spoke much of their summer hunting excursions on the Pamirs and the neighbouring hills in pursuit of large game, chiefly the *Ovis poli* and ibex. He was accompanied by a number of men with hawks and dogs. Among the dogs were a pair of ibex hounds, two spaniels from Kolab, and a terrier nondescript from Chitral, but looking uncommonly like an importation from the British infantry quarter of Peshawur. The ibex hounds appeared to me to be merely the Persian greyhound, with a longer and thicker coat from being born and bred in the colder country of Wakhan. They are used in the chase merely as an aid to the hunter. When ibex are found near precipitous cliffs, the passage from which can be so occupied by a few men as to prevent escape, the dogs are let loose and the ibex generally take to the rocks, where, ascending to the farthest points, they become almost paralysed with alarm, and fall an easy prey to the matchlockmen, who follow them up till within easy shot. Dogs are similarly used for ibex-shooting in Upper Chitral, as observed by Mr. Hayward in 1869, and also in the Wardwan district of Kashmir. Ali Murdan Shah told me that his ibex hounds had no chance with *Ovis poli*, which always escape from them with ease if not wounded. The hawks are used against the "chikor" (hill partridge) which is found throughout the lower valleys. This bird is met with from the lower Himalayahs adjoining the plains of Hindustan, to the southern slopes of the Tian Shan range. An old man among the attendants of the "Mirzada" remembered Wood the traveller well, having been at Langar Kisht when he passed through on his way to the Great Pamir in 1838.

KILA PANJA ON THE OXUS - LOOKING EAST

We reached Sarhadd at the seventh day from Sirikol, and Kila Panja on the twelfth. The extreme severity of the weather compelled us to make short journeys the first three days from Sarhadd. A violent and blinding snowstorm met us each day on the march, accompanied by a wind so intense in its coldness as to freeze the driven snowflakes on our faces. On the fourth day we encamped at Zong, a large village on the right bank of the Oxus, immediately below the junction of the Great and Little Pamir streams. We reached Kila Panja on the following day, the 13th of April. Mir Futteh Ali Shah rode out to meet us, and conducted us to our camp, which was pitched on an open plain in the close vicinity of his fort. The Mir was an old man of tall form and good face, but feeble from age and infirmity. He welcomed us to Wakhan, and expressed himself in the usual Oriental complimentary terms as happy to see us at Kila Panja.

Kila Panja is on the left bank of the Oxus (or the Panja as it is there called), about five miles below the junction of the two Pamir streams. The place is so called from five forts which stand together there. Only two, however, can properly be styled forts even according to local notions, the other three being merely towers planted on high upstanding rocks in their vicinity. The principal fort is occupied by the Mir; it is an irregular building of stone and mud, with high walls and many towers, situated on an eminence close to the river. We found the river about sixty yards broad and easily fordable; when in flood it is crossed by means of inflated skin rafts.

We visited the Mir in his fort in the evening. We were received in a centre room with a roof opening to act as both chimney and window, and spaces on the four sides, exactly

similar in style to the village houses, but larger and higher.
The entrance was, as with them, through the stables. The Mir
received us attended by many of the "Aksakals" (elders) of
the people. There was no attempt at display of any kind, the
chief being dressed in the plainest manner possible, his people
likewise, and the room comfortless in the extreme. Everything
was rough except manners, which were good to a degree. We
observed what we had seen before with the Mirzada, respect
paid by kissing the hand; the people kissing the Mir's hand on
arrival, on departure, and on receiving an order.

Futteh Ali Shah* was a younger brother of Muhammad Rahim, who was Mir when Wood visited Wakhan.
The family claims descent from Alexander of Macedon; and
Futteh Ali Shah said that the ruling families of Chitral, Shighnan, and other neighbouring states spring from his; but this, I
imagine, is what each says of all the others who similarly trace
their ancestry to the great Sikandar. Muhammad Rahim was
succeeded by a cousin who only ruled one year, when Futteh
Ali Shah seized the Mirship, which he has held ever since, a
period of thirty-five years. He was full of information, and
told us much during our frequent meetings at Kila Panja. He
appeared to have much influence over his people, and to be
regarded by them with great deference and respect. He was
believed by them to be a magician, and one of the first questions
he asked about us was if we could do anything wonderful in
magic. He was on excellent terms with the rulers of Shighnan
and Kunjut, and this caused the peace to be kept by their
subjects towards each other, while the Atalik's reputation for

* Mir Futteh Ali Shah died about nine months after our visit.

Khan assuming the deputy-governorship. The tribute consisted of two camels, twelve horses, twelve cows, and twelve blankets, and this has been fixed as the yearly due from Wakhan. The Mir said to me "No money is asked, for the country has none." He spoke bitterly of the cruel exactions made by the Badakhshi Mirs, and said that he greatly preferred the Affghans as masters.

Mir Futteh Ali Shah took part with the Atalik and Buzurg Khan in the siege of Kashghar, and was engaged in the battle of Kanarik in 1865. He commanded a Wakhi force which, with a Badakhshi contingent, crossed the Great Pamir in the summer of that year, and proceeded to Kashghar by the Tagharma plain and Bas Robat route. A Tungani flag, taken at Kanarik, was shown to us at Kila Panja as a trophy of that battle.

The number of inhabitants in Wakhan is said to have greatly decreased during latter years. One thousand families were spoken of as its former population, but now there are not more than five hundred, giving a total of about three thousand souls. There is a large colony of Wakhis in the Sanju district of Yarkand, and fifty families are said to have emigrated to the Sirikol valley during the reign of Mir Futteh Ali Shah. The people, as a rule, are very poor, but they have the reputation of being avaricious and particularly fond of money. They resemble the Sirikolis in appearance, and like them believe themselves to be descended from wanderers who assembled and settled in Wakhan, from many quarters. They are Shiah Muhammadans, and acknowledge Aga Khan of Bombay as their spiritual head, to whom they annually send offerings of one-tenth of all produce of their flocks and lands. This payment is also made by the people of the neighbouring states and districts of Shighnan, Roshan, Chitral, Munjan, and Sanglig.

The snow-storms which prevailed during our first five days in Wakhan compelled us sometimes to seek shelter in the houses of the villagers, where we had several opportunities of observing their domestic life. The houses are flat-roofed and built of stone and mud. The outer enclosed rooms are used as stables for horses and cattle. The family occupy one large centre room, which has an opening immediately above an oven-like fireplace sunk in the middle of the floor. On the four sides round this room are raised platform sleeping places, one of which is partly enclosed, and allotted to the women and children. The men are warlike, hardy, and enduring; they are all given to field sports, and appear fond of arms. Every house showed the arms of its male occupants slung on the walls. The principal arm is the long rifled matchlock with the forked rest, in general use throughout Turkistan. The women are delicate-looking, considering the wild mountain country in which they live; they do not veil, and appear to have more control in the household than is usual in the East. We observed the same, in this respect, among the Kirghiz. Whenever a present was given in return for shelter and hospitality, the female head of the house was generally called to receive it. The men do all the field work, the women being left to manage all about the house. The Wakhis as a people are good looking, and many faces of extreme regularity of feature were seen. Fair hair and blue eyes are not uncommon. They all speak Persian, besides their own peculiar dialect. Their dress is somewhat similar to that of the Sirikolis, the men wearing long robes of home-spun woollen stuffs, and sheepskin coats, and the women having white cotton garments, with a narrow piece of cotton rolled flat round the head. The men who can afford the luxury affect the pointed Affghan coloured cap with the usual blue and white checked turban.

The majority of the inhabitants move with their flocks and herds in summer to grazing grounds on the heights in their neighbourhood. A few people remain in each village to attend to the growing crops, which are harvested on the return from the summer pasture lands. The flocks and herds consist of sheep and goats, cattle and yaks. The horses of the country are small, hardy, and well bred. Wheat, huskless barley, beans and peas, are the principal crops in Wakhan. Melons and apricots ripen at Zong, near Kila Panja. The climate of the Sarhadd district, for thirty-five miles down from the first village at the head of the valley, is too cold for wheat. The only timber grown is the white poplar, and that, by reason of the violent winds of the country, requires a sheltered position. Stunted red willow and other hardy bush woods are plentiful in the sandy stretches along the river banks. There appears to be no mineral wealth in Wakhan. Salt of a very inferior quality and iron are procured from Badakhshan. We found great difficulty in getting horse-shoes or iron to make them, and it was only by working up some iron tent-pegs, a ploughshare, and a cooking pot, that we were able to complete the number required for our return journey over the Great Pamir.

The present trade between Eastern and Western Turkistan is small. It consists chiefly of "churrus" (intoxicating drug) and cotton cloth of Khoten and Yarkand manufacture from the former, and of horses, indigo, kincob, and sundries from the latter. The indigo and kincob are obtained from India. The Mir of Wakhan levies transit-dues at a uniform rate of one Muhammad-shahi rupee (equal to about two shillings and four-pence) per horse load, irrespective of value. No dues are levied for Kashghar at Sirikol, this being done on the goods reaching their destination. •The Badakhshan currency is the coin of Wakhan, but there is very little of it in the country, and almost all trade transactions are effected by barter. We found the Mir at the time of our arrival in great straits for the means to satisfy a merciless creditor, who had come from Badakhshan to press a claim for a sum equivalent to about £45. Payment in the form of the precious metals was wanted, and we were in need of provisions to a considerable extent daily, as well as a stock for our farther journey, and the use of a large number of horses to carry it; so in return for all, our gold was given at this opportune time to relieve Wakhan of its state debt.

Carrotty-haired Sirikoli attendant of Alif Beg's

KAFFIR FORT NEAR HISSAR-WAKHAN.

CHAPTER X.

WAKHAN—FRIENDLY RELATIONS WITH KUNJUT—PEOPLE OF KUNJUT—SHIGHNAN FRIENDLY WITH WAKHAN—MY MESSENGER TO SHIGHNAN—SHORT ACCOUNT OF COUNTRY—MURGHAB (GREAT KARAKUL) RIVER—RUBY MINES—SHIAH SECT—KAFIR FORTS—MIR WALI SUPPOSED MURDERER OF MR. HAYWARD—YASSIN—ALIF BEG OF SIRIKOL—SLAVERY.

FUTTEH ALI SHAH was closely connected with Ghazan Khan, the chief of Hunza, to whose sister he had long been married, and to whom he lately gave one of his own daughters in marriage. Ali Murdan Shah, the eldest son, was said to be the nephew of the Kunjut chief. He always appeared with a following of Kunjutis, and told me that he made a yearly visit to Hunza, generally staying there several months. The journey from Kila Panja occupies from eight to ten days, and the paths and passes are described as rough and difficult. The best road leads up the stream which joins the Little Pamir one at Langar, and crosses by the Kura pass, which, however, is closed by snow for three months in winter. The road which branches off from the Little Pamir one higher up is open throughout the year, but is not passable by horses. The Kunjutis are Shiah Muhammadans, but they are little trammelled by their religious obligations, as shown by their free indulgence in wine, music, and dancing. Wine is made from the grape and mulberry, which grow luxuriantly in the deep warm sheltered ravines of Kunjut. They send no offerings to their spiritual chief, Aga Khan, as their co-religionists in the neighbourhood do. The country of Kunjut is divided between the two small states of Hunza and Nagar, both of which have latterly been, more or less, in a state of hostility to each other. The people are alike in character and religion. They have an evil reputation with their neighbours as robbers and man-stealers, treacherous, cruel, and cowardly.

The relations between Wakhan and Shighnan are of the most friendly nature, and have been so for a long time. Futteh Ali Shah mentioned having visited the Shah of Shighnan five times during past years. Desiring to obtain further knowledge of the course of the Oxus, advantage was taken of the friendship existing between these chiefs to send Captain Trotter's intelligent assistant surveyor, under Futteh Ali Shah's protection, with a complimentary letter and present to Eusuf Ali Khan of Shighnan. This explorer proceeded as far as Wamur, passing along about 100 miles of the unknown portion of the river northwards from Ishkashim. He was well received by Eusuf Ali at Wamur, and the following information about the country in that direction is taken from his account. The ruler of Shighnan claims the title of Shah. The present Shah, Eusuf Ali, rules over both Shighnan and Roshan. One of his sisters is married to the Amir of Kashghar, another to Muhammad Alum Khan, the Affghan governor of Balkh and Badakhshan, and a third to Khodayar Khan of Khokand (the ruler lately driven out by an insurrection of the people). The country of Shighnan and Roshan is sometimes called Zujan (two-lived), its climate and water being considered so good that a man on entering it is said to have come into the possession of two lives. Bar Panja, the capital of Shighnan, containing about 1500 houses, stands on the left bank, and Wamur, the capital of Roshan, on the right bank of the Oxus; but the greater portion of both countries is on the right bank. The Murghab, also known as the Bartang river, joins the Panja at Wamur, and is there larger in volume and more rapid in current than the latter. The united streams retain the name of Panja carried from Wakhan, till Kolab is reached, after which it is known as the Amu or Hamu. The Murghab may, however, be considered the largest and longest of all the affluents of the Oxus. The Suchan, formed by two large streams, the Shakh-Darrah and the Ghund, joins the Panja from the east nearly opposite Bar Panja. The men are great sportsmen, and all, even to the Shah, play on horseback at "chaugan" (the polo of that part), but with larger horses and longer sticks than are used in Ladak. The ball, moreover, is a soft leather one. Among the game animals are the *Ovis poli*, ibex, and a small antelope. Much wine is made and drunk in the country. It is a red sweet liquor produced from the cherry. There are now about 4700 houses or families in Shighnan and Roshan together, but the population is said to have been much greater in former times. Shighnan and Roshan used to receive from the Chinese, during their occupation of Eastern Turkistan, a yearly payment similar to that made to Sirikol, Kunjut, and

Wakhan, for the protection of the frontier and the trade routes. The ruby mines of Gharan are now being worked under the orders of Sher Ali, the Amir of Kabul. It was said that one large ruby the size of a pigeon's egg, as well as some smaller ones, were found lately and sent to the Amir. The working of these mines appears to be attended with considerable risk and great hardship.

According to Shighni accounts, the family of the Shah of Shighnan originally came from Persia, and the first arrival from that country (said to have been between 500 and 700 years ago) was the Shah-i-Khamosh, who was a Syud and a Fakir. The country was at that time in the hands of the Zardushtis (ancient Guebers—fire-worshippers), a powerful and learned race. The Shah-i-Khamosh commenced to teach these people the Koran. There were already at this time Musulmans in the neighbouring country of Darwaz, and many of them flocked into Shighnan as followers of the Shah-i-Khamosh. In about ten years he had converted large numbers of the people, and a religious war commenced, which ended in this leader wresting the kingdom from Kahakah, the ruler of Shighnan and Roshan under the Zardushtis, the seat of whose government was then at Balkh. After this the teaching of the people continued, and in ten years more all had been converted to the Shiah form of the Muhammadan faith.

If this be true it is probable that proselytising expeditions were sent into Wakhan and the neighbouring hill countries, and extended their operations even to Sirikol and Kunjut, gaining all over to the Shiah faith which they now profess. The ruins of three forts, said by the natives to have been erected by the "Atash-parastan" (fire-worshippers), still exist in Wakhan: one called

"Kahkaha" in the Ishtrak district; another named "Maichun" in the vicinity of Khandut; and the third, Kila Sangibar, close to the hamlet of Hissar. The first was the residence of the ruler of the Zardushtis, and is said to bear signs of having been better built than the others. It consisted of a single square building of stone and lime, situated close to the Panja and on its right bank. The "Maichun" ruins show stone walls rising successively one above the other, with a space of about 200 yards between them. These walls are made of rough stone and lime. A stone causeway, still in good preservation, leads to the upper fort from the bank of the Panja. The lower wall is entirely in ruins, but all the others are in good condition; the facing of the walls is bound with lime. Within the upper fort is an oval-shaped space of level ground, about 150 paces long and 75 wide, originally containing houses, of which no vestige now remains. The fort at Hissar is built on a solitary rock standing out high on the plain, near the junction of the two Pamir streams, and is said to be of very ancient date. We examined the ruins, and found them to show no signs of greater antiquity or of having been more remarkable than the Tashkurgan (stone-fort) of Sirikol. The mud used as cement in the walls indicated no great age. No hewn stones were seen in the whole place, and neither in it nor the other ruins are inscriptions of any sort to be found.

Resaidar Muhammad Afzul Khan, who was sent on to Wakhan to prepare for our arrival there, found the Mir at first reluctant to receive us. A report had gone abroad that the real object of our visit was to seize and carry off Mir Wali Khan, the alleged murderer of Mr. Hayward, who was then residing at Kila Panja. Mr. Hayward, the bold and adventurous traveller, who penetrated to Kashghar in 1868 at the same time as Mr. Shaw, was disappointed in his design of passing thence to the Pamir, and on his return to Kashmir determined to make the attempt by the Gilgit and Yassin (Upper Chitral) route. He visited Yassin in the spring of 1870, and formed the acquaintance of Wali Khan, the Mir of the place. He found the Darkote pass leading over the Hindu Kush range to Wakhan and the basin of the Oxus closed with snow, and went back to India, after arranging with Mir Wali, the chief, to return in summer, and cross to Wakhan with his assistance. He came back again in July of the same year, and was brutally murdered by Mir Wali, acting under the Chitral chief's orders, in Yassin territory, at the foot of the Darkote pass, about twenty miles from Sarhadd, Wakhan. All Mr. Hayward's servants and followers were murdered at the same time as their master, with the exception of his Munshi (writer), who was spared to be made use of, but was afterwards put to death, at Chitral it is said. Poor Mr. Hayward was believed to be in possession of a considerable amount of gold and valuable presents for the chiefs beyond Yassin, and the desire to obtain these, as well as the Chitral ruler's wish to take the traveller's life, appears to have induced Mir Wali to commit this infamous act. Aman-ul-Mulk, the Chitral ruler and father-in-law of Mir Wali, on hearing of the indignation the crime had caused, promptly expressed his intention to slay his son-in-law, and despatched a force to seize him. Mir Wali fled to Wakhan, where he obtained protection from Mir Futteh Ali Shah. His Mirship was confiscated and conferred on his cousin Pahlvan Khan, a nephew of Aman-ul-Mulk. Mir Wali, after a short stay in Wakhan, went to Chitral, and presenting himself before his father-in-law, begged for his life for his wife's sake.

He remained with Aman-ul-Mulk for about two years, when having rendered him the hideous service of murdering an obnoxious nephew, he was rewarded by reinstatement as Mir of Yassin, displacing Pahlvan Khan, who about the same time had been similarly engaged in ridding himself of his half-brother, Ghazi Khan, whom he suspected of intriguing to supplant him.

Mir Wali ruled in Yassin after this but a little over a year, when Pahlvan Khan was restored to favour, and was a second time sent by Aman-ul-Mulk with a force to capture and kill Mir Wali, who, however, as before, received timely information and escaped to Wakhan. Mir Wali on this occasion was accompanied in his flight by a great number of Yassini families, numbering about one thousand souls, who feared the return of Pahlvan Khan, and preferred exile with their hereditary chief. These people were distributed in the villages of Wakhan, and continue to reside there. Aman-ul-Mulk has several times demanded the surrender of these Yassinis, but Futteh Ali Shah declined to give them up, leaving the matter of return to their own choice. They, however, dread and dislike the Chitralis too much to desire to go back.

Mir Wali succeeded his father thirteen years ago. About three years previously the father of Aman-ul-Mulk made an attempt to subjugate Yassin, and invaded the country with a force, but was repulsed by Mir Wali's father. The Chitral ruler died shortly after, and was succeeded by his son now in power. Friendship was re-established between Yassin and Chitral, but on the death of Mir Wali's father Aman-ul-Mulk advanced with a force and renewed the old claim to Mastuch and Yassin. Mir Wali submitted without a struggle, and was permitted to retain the Mirship on agreeing to the Chitral terms. His dependence was further secured by receiving in marriage a daughter of Aman-ul-Mulk. Pahlvan Khan was appointed Mir of Mastuch.

Mir Futteh Ali Shah asserted that Aman-ul-Mulk ordered Mir Wali to murder Mr. Hayward, threatening him with death in case of disobedience, and on this ground he regarded Mir Wali as comparatively guiltless. He held that Mir Wali, as the vassal, was exonerated by the order of his feudal lord, and that the latter is alone to blame. He therefore pitied, he said, Mir Wali in his misfortune, and gave him and his people "shelter and bread" when they asked of him. He added that Aman-ul-Mulk took the plunder and burdened Mir Wali with the shame. We have other evidence also of the Chitral ruler's possession of the ill-fated traveller's property.

Mr. Hayward's rifles were breech-loaders, and we gathered from what we saw and heard at Panja, that these, in being handled and shown as curiosities in firearms by his murderers, had caused two serious and fatal accidents. The old Mir asked to see our weapons, and on my offering to put a breech-loading rifle into his hands and to show him how to open the breech and load, he drew back with alarm, saying that they in Wakhan did not understand such "guns," that in their hands they were dangerous even to one's friends; and he then mentioned that such another gun, on being shown at Panja some time before, had exploded and severely wounded a man, and that the same thing had happened under similar circumstances at Zebak, the gun again exploding there and killing the brother of the man who held it, besides wounding another so badly that he died shortly after. Other matters also conduced to the belief that the only breech-loading arms previously seen at Panja were poor Hayward's, taken by Mir Wali on his flight from Yassin and subsequent journey to Chitral *via* Zebak, when they passed into the possession of his father-in-law Aman-ul-Mulk.

Mir Wali was at Kila Panja while we journeyed over, and we heard at Sirikol that he regarded our expected visit with considerable anxiety, and we afterwards found that Mir Futteh Ali Shah had shared this anxiety, believing that evil might result to himself for having given an asylum to him who was the instrument of the murder of one of our countrymen. He stated his fears in public, saying, " I have incurred the displeasure of the Atalik for sheltering Alif Beg of Sirikol, and now I am threatened with the anger of the English for giving protection to Mir Wali." This was repeated to Mir Wali, who, after proving his innocence, according to their notions of rude feudalism, by showing the order under which he acted in murdering Mr. Hayward, left for Faizabad, Badakhshan, before our arrival.

Alif Beg, the ex-ruler of Sirikol, was residing with the Mir of Wakhan during our stay at Kila Panja, and paid me a visit two days previous to our departure. A report had been spread that the Kashgharis in our camp intended with our assistance to take him by force to Sirikol, and he had accordingly been in a state of alarm for some days after our arrival. On the conviction becoming general that the rumours concerning us were false, he determined to make our acquaintance. He carried out his intention, however, in a manner which showed that he had not entirely set aside all fear and suspicion. He came to my tent without giving any notice, and entering abruptly, shook hands, informing me, in reply to my question, that he was Alif Beg. He sat all the time of his visit with his hand resting on a pistol in his belt, while one of his followers stood guard at the tent door with a gun on his shoulder. He conversed with me for a long time about Sirikol and the neighbouring countries. He had lately returned from a visit to some of the garrison towns of Russian Turkistan, and he talked much of what he had seen there. His sister, who was a widow of the late ruler of Shighnan and Roshan, is married to Ali Murdan Shah of Wakhan.

Slavery still continues to be the curse of many of the Shiah states round about Badakhshan. Notwithstanding its prohibition by the Amir of Kabul, the disgraceful trade in human beings, with all its attendant crime and cruelty, still flourishes. A man has about the same value as a woman, and the selling-price of a slave is from £12 to £18, or ten to fifteen bullocks, five to eight yaks, or two Kirghiz guns. The open slave-market certainly is closed, but beyond that nothing seemingly is done to suppress the shameful and horrible traffic, which is otherwise carried on as briskly as ever. The Affghan occupation of Badakhshan has had the good effect of abolishing the tribute in slaves which used to be demanded and enforced by the ruling Suni Mirs from their feudatories with subjects professing the heretical Shiah creed. Futteh Ali Shah of Wakhan told me that the tribute he paid in September 1873 was the first ever given of which slaves did not form a part. Muhammad Khan, the late ruler of Shighnan, is said to have sold great numbers of his subjects into slavery during his short reign of four years. He died in 1869, and was succeeded by the present Shah, Eusuf Ali, who not only discontinued the enslaving of the people, but also refused to give any as slaves in the tribute to Badakhshan. The tribute is now paid in horses. It was reported that during the absence of Mir Wali many of the inhabitants of Yassin and Mastuch had been sold into slavery by order of Aman-ul-Mulk, the ruler of Chitral, and that one merchant alone had lately taken away nearly a hundred slaves. When Mir Wali was in Balkh during our visit to Wakhan, he told the governor of Badakhshan that many of his subjects were being brought into the country as slaves, and obtained permission to attack the slave-merchants for the purpose of rescuing them. Mir Wali fell upon a slave party at Zebak in the end of May, and recovered many of his people.

Both the Great and Little Pamirs have remained unvisited for summer pasture by Kirghiz or Wakhis for a long time now, solely on account of the feuds, raids, and reprisals caused by the slave traffic. Kidnapping Kunjutis and Kirghiz, Shignis and Wakhis, attacked and harried one another to that extent that the open country was abandoned, and each kept to their own confined valleys. Avarice and greed urged Shiah even to steal Shiah, for sale to the Suni, who considers the enslaving of the "accursed Rafizi" a meritorious act, giving the heretic an opportunity of benefiting by example, and being rescued from perdition by conversion to the orthodox faith. In those days traders could only cross the Pamirs in numerous well-armed bands, but all that violent state of things has since changed to one of peace and security. Merchants now pass and repass at all seasons in small parties without molestation, and the neighbouring states do their utmost to prevent any return to the old condition of violence and lawlessness. I have already mentioned an instance of the readiness with which international complaints between subjects of Wakhan and Kashghar are listened to, and wrongs redressed. The Atalik's reputation for prompt and severe action in all cases of disorder and disturbance by his own subjects or his neighbours' has done much to bring about this improvement, and shows the great good already proceeding from the establishment of his strong government among rude unsettled small states unable or unwilling of themselves to control their subjects to the satisfaction of others.

WAKHI FALCONER WITH YOUNG HAWK.

YOL MAZAR (ROADSIDE SHRINE) ON THE GREAT PAMIR BRANCH OF THE OXUS.

CHAPTER XI.

SEVERE WEATHER—SUPPLIES—SNOW ON GREAT PAMIR—SIGNS OF SPRING—DEPARTURE FOR GREAT PAMIR — CAPTAIN BIDDULPH GOES TO THE CHITRAL PASSES — ALI MURDAN SHAH'S SIGNET RING — KIRGHIZ OF GREAT PAMIR — ROAD — WOOD'S VICTORIA LAKE—GREAT PAMIR WATERSHED—DEEP SNOW—PAMIR PATHS—CAPTAIN BIDDULPH REJOINS—ALICHOR AND SIRIZ PAMIRS—RANG KUL—TASHKURGAN ON SIRIZ PAMIR—WILD ANIMALS—GIGANTIC PAIR OF *OVIS POLI* HORNS—RAREFACTION OF THE AIR—LOCAL NAME OF LAKE VICTORIA—GENERAL DESCRIPTION OF THE PAMIR PLATEAU—MEANING OF "PAMIR"—HOT SPRINGS—"BOLOR"—AKTASH—SHORT SUPPLIES—DIFFICULT DEFILE—RETURN TO SIRIKOL.

WE remained thirteen days at Kila Panja. The weather was very severe most of that time. Snow fell on six days, and an intensely cold wind blew regularly till within three days of our departure. Wood speaks in his *Journey to the Source of the Oxus* of the withering blast of the " bad-i-Wakhan " (wind of Wakhan), blowing down the valley. This wind prevailed during a great part of our stay at Panja, and only ceased occasionally, to be followed by an equally chilling wind from the opposite direction, Badakhshan. These winds swept across the open plain on which we were encamped with a cutting violence which made our tent life there rather miserable at times.

Our party was a large one, amounting, with our Sepoy guard of five men of the Guide Corps, and a similar number of Kashgharis, to forty-eight men, with seventy-two horses. We had arrived at the most unfavourable time of the year for supplies, most of the excess above the wants of the inhabitants being sold in the end of summer and during the autumn to the merchants who pass with their "kafilas" about that time. The matter of our daily supplies, and a sufficiency to take us back over the Pamir, was one of considerable difficulty.

We had been told that the Great Pamir, on account of snow, is rarely passable till the end of June, and were assured that it would be impossible for a large party like ours to succeed in any attempt to cross it earlier. On the 15th April I despatched a Sepoy of the Guides with two of the Mir's men towards the Great Pamir lake to report on the depth of snow, so that we might take advantage of any possible chance of passage that way. They returned in eight days, bringing such an account of the road as induced us to determine on trying it. They found the snow deep and heavy in the drifts and hollows, but the fact of their having been able to reach the lake made us regard the journey as less difficult than had been previously represented. The Mir visited us the day after the return of the guides, and referring to their report, said that he would give all assistance in his power to gratify our desire to see the Great Pamir lake, and go back by a different route from that by which we came. Our baggage horses had not recovered from the severe effects of the journey over, but the Mir gave us the use of several fresh animals, to allow of occasional relief to those which had suffered most. The Mir also made arrangements for the provision and carriage of eight days' supply of food and grain for men and horses on the return journey.

Ploughing and flooding of the fields to facilitate the breaking up of the ground in preparation for sowing were commenced during our stay at Kila Panja. The streams of the side ravines issuing from the glaciers and deep snow-beds of the high ranges which rise from the valley here, principally the Hindu Kush on the southern side, give an abundant water-supply for irrigation purposes throughout the summer, which, with the extreme regularity of the season in this country of scanty rainfall, enables the inhabitants to reckon very confidently on an unfailing harvest. On the 25th the weather changed suddenly from cold to mild, and a fall of rain that night, succeeded by a warm day without wind, gave sure sign of coming spring.

On the 26th we paid a farewell visit to the Mir, and left Kila Panja; Dr. Stoliczka, Captain Trotter, and myself, for the Great Pamir, and Captain Biddulph, accompanied by Resaidar Muhammad Afzal Khan, for the Little Pamir, a spot in the Aktash valley being appointed as our rendezvous on the 4th of May.

We (the Great Pamir party) halted the first day at Langar Kisht, a considerable village on the right bank of the Great Pamir stream, and about two miles above its junction with that of the Little Pamir. It is the last village in the valley leading to the lake. The Mir's son, Ali Murdan Shah, visited us in the evening to say good-bye, and present a pair of ibex-hounds, which were evidently considered a valuable gift. The sporting tastes of the Wakhis lead them not to regard the dog as a mean animal as other Muhammadans do. Wood mentions how a man slave was exchanged for a dog, and the Mir, when we took leave of him, said that he would be always glad to see our countrymen, and that even a dog of theirs would be welcomed, and he would himself rise in the night time to see food cooked for it. On asking Ali Murdan Shah at parting what he wished particularly to be sent from India as a memento of our visit, he requested a signet ring, similar to my own, with the following couplet engraved on it in the Persian character :—

> Ba fazl-i-an Khudawind-i-nigahban
> Ali Murdan ghulam-i-Shah-i-Murdan.
>
> By the grace of the Protecting Lord,
> Ali Murdan, the servant of the King of Men.

The excellence of the Delhi engravers' work is well known beyond our Indian frontier, and the Mirzada was gladdened in due course by the receipt of a perfect specimen of their handicraft in the manner he desired.

The ring was included in the presents sent to the Mir on our return to India, and was used by the son in his reply to my letter which accompanied it.

From Langar Kisht our road lay in a general north-easterly direction, at some height along the slopes of the mountains on the right bank of the stream. The mountains on each side rise in a very gradual incline from the deep rocky gorge in which the stream flows. The Zerzamin and Mutz streams join from the north at eight and nineteen miles from Langar Kisht. The upper or summer road to Shighnan leads along the latter. Bar Panja, the capital, is said to be reached in eight days by it, and Shakh-Darrah in three. Shakh-Darrah was at one time a small independent Mirship, but it is now absorbed in Shighnan. The Kirghiz who formerly occupied the winter villages, the ruins of which we saw in sheltered spots towards the western end of the Great Pamir, are now located in Shakh-Darrah, and make the Alichor Pamir their summer pasture resort. According to the Wakhis, the Mutz stream has a course of about twenty-five miles, rising near the crest of the mountain range to the north which forms the boundary between Wakhan and Shighnan.

The Great Pamir appears to begin twenty-five miles above Langar Kisht. The valley is narrow up to that point, with the base of the mountains touching the bed of the stream, but it there opens out, and the hills show low and rounded. Thence the road lay in the same general north-easterly direction, over flats and long easy slopes the whole way to the lake. Birch and willow are plentiful to within twenty-five miles of the lake, and from that on, the never-failing wild lavender plant affords a sufficient supply of fuel. Excellent grass, similar to that of the Little Pamir and the Aktash and Sirikol valleys, is found throughout. The partially frozen and extremely low state of the stream facilitated our journey, by allowing us to pass over its surface, and along its bed at places where later in the season the increased flow of water necessitates a higher path being followed. We saw snow pheasants and hares west of the lake, and wild fowl all along the stream up to its source. The lake stream in the first sixteen miles of its course flows between high gravelly banks, which rise to far-extending downs, dying away in the long and easy mountain slopes. We were remarkably fortunate in meeting with comparatively little snow as far as the lake. There was a considerable fall on the night of the 29th at our camp, twenty-five miles below the lake.

VICTORIA LAKE, GREAT PAM'R, LOOKING W

GREAT PAMIR (VICTORIA) LAKE—EASTERN END.

We reached the Great Pamir or Wood's Lake on 1st May. It was entirely frozen over, and covered with a thin coating of snow. Its water is perfectly fresh, judging from what we used for two days high up from the stream which flows out of it. It extends east and west, and is about ten miles long by three broad. The water-marks on the shores, however, indicated a considerable enlargement in summer. The southern shore is even, the northern broken and irregular. Many signs of considerable depth were observed. At three miles from the foot a high promontory runs out from the northern shore and approaches the southern side to within less than a mile. The hills to the south slope very gradually from the edge of the lake, and the peaks rise to a height of four or five thousand feet above it. Broad plains and low undulations for about three miles lie between it and the hills to the north, which appear much lower than those to the south. Captain Trotter made the lake to be 13,900 feet above the sea.

The valley closes in at the head of the lake, and continues narrow for about eight miles, when it again opens out with a steady fall to the east. Captain Trotter, by close examination, made the watershed to be at this point 14,300 feet. Two small frozen lakes were observed near the head of the lake, under the high snowy mountains which close in there from the south. They presented the appearance of ice accumulations, and probably, after furnishing feeders to the lake for a short time, finally disappear in summer. A valley at the head of the lake leads to the Wurm pass over the southern range, by which the Little Pamir, Langar, and Sarhadd are reached in one and two days respectively.

There was a great deal of snow about the lake, and it lay so deep on the high ground at its head, and in the valley leading down east from the watershed, that the easy regular road that way could not be followed. We were accordingly forced to seek a path along the low hills to the north, and had considerable difficulty in forcing our way through the heavy snow-drifts. The snow ceased about eighteen miles from the lake. The eastern stream from the watershed is there joined by one from Shash-Darrah (six valleys) in the range between the Great and Little Pamirs. Several paths lead from this point to the Little Pamir and the Aktash valley. We followed the united stream, here called the Isligh, down to the Aktash valley, a distance of fifty-eight miles, over a gentle fall the whole way. The hills right and left there are low and rounded, with great openings and depressions appearing everywhere. We were accompanied by a large party of Wakhis, acting as guides, and in charge of the horses carrying our supplies. On one of the guides being asked if paths lay in the direction of certain

THE AKTASH ROCK IN THE AKTASH VALLEY – LOOKING S.E. – ICE BREAKING UP ON THE AKSU

openings pointed out; the answer was, "Yes, there are paths all over the Pamir; it has a thousand roads; with a guide you can go in all directions." We reckoned the length of the Great Pamir from its western limit to the Aktash valley to be 108 miles, with an average breadth of about three miles. We travelled eighteen miles south-east up the Aktash valley, to the halting-place which had been agreed upon with Captain Biddulph as the place of meeting on 4th May. Both parties reached punctually on that date, we marching thirty-seven miles to keep the engagement. The ice was then breaking up on the Aksu, and we had some difficulty in finding a safe crossing-place on its frozen surface.

Captain Biddulph succeeded in his lovely journey by the Little Pamir route, and made valuable additions to the results of our exploration work. The snow, which lay deep when we all passed over to Wakhan, had almost entirely disappeared by the time he returned, and the lake outlet, with the flow of its stream, the Aksu, was again carefully examined and noted.

The Alichor Pamir runs east and west, almost parallel to the Great and Little Pamirs. According to Wakhi accounts, it is similar in character to them, broad at the eastern and narrow at the western end. It is connected with the Great Pamir by the "Dasht-i-Khargoshi," a desert flat twenty miles long, which extends across from a point about twenty miles west of Wood's Lake. A road passes along it and branches from the Alichor to Shighnan and Khokand. A stagnant lake called "Tuz" and "Sussik Kul" (salt putrid lake) lies near the western end of the Alichor. The water of it was described to me as being salt to the taste. The native traveller, Abdul Mejid, noticed this lake as at the first stage from Khargoshi on his way to Khokand, but some lingering doubts concerning it led to the idea that possibly Wood's Lake was meant, and that its water was brackish. Our evidence, however, confirms the accuracy of Colonel Yule's opinion, that it was " difficult to conceive that a lake with so copious an effluent as it (Wood's lake) should have salt waters." East of the Sussik Kul a fresh-water stream rises and flows into the Yeshil Kul (green lake), lower down in the Alichor, from which another stream issues and joins the Murghab, below its junction with the Aksu. The Kashgharis who fled with the Khojas in the last century, before the Chinese when they took possession of Eastern Turkistan, passed up the Alichor Pamir in their flight to Badakhshan. They were overtaken by a pursuing Chinese force near the Yeshil Kul, and are said to have driven their women and children, mounted on camels and horses, into the lake, to meet their death by drowning rather than they should fall into the hands of the enemy. The Kirghiz have a legend that the sounds of lamentation, and of people and animals in terror of death, are often heard near the lake.

I have already mentioned the Siriz Pamir when speaking of the Aktash valley. This Pamir appears to be a continuation of the Aktash valley, similarly as the Little Pamir is, and as the Taghdungbash is of the Sirikol valley. It seems to run from Ak-Balik in the east to Bartang in the west. Bartang is the beginning of inhabited and cultivated Shighnan in that direction. It is described as abounding with fruit-bearing trees, and must therefore be much lower than Kila Panja, with a very different climate. It is easy to believe this, when the long course of the Aksu-Murghab, with a steady fall, is considered.

The Kirghiz spoke of the Rang (Ibex) Kul, a large lake about one day's journey from Ak-Balik, and situated in the Siriz Pamir. This probably is the Rang Kul of Pamir Khurd, mentioned in Colonel Yule's Essay on the Geography of the Oxus, the Aktash valley being there regarded as the Little Pamir, of which it is but the continuation, as I have already explained. By the Kirghiz accounts, the Great Karakul is four days', the Little Karakul three, the Rang Kul one, the Yeshil Kul two and a half, and Bartang four days' journey from Ak-Balik. I estimate the day's journey in these accounts at fifteen miles in a direct line. The Tagharma Kirghiz told me of the ruins of an old "Tashkurgan" (stone fort) near Ak-Balik similar to that in the Sirikol valley.

The animals of the Pamirs are the *Ovis poli*, ibex, brown bear, leopard, lynx, wolf, fox, marmot, and hare. These remain throughout the year. Wild fowl swarm on the lakes in summer. The wild yak is not known on or near the Pamirs. We were not fortunate in pursuit of game. We saw a great many *Ovis poli*, but on the way over to Wakhan the snow lay too deep to permit of sport, and on the journey back our limited supplies would not admit of a halt for the purpose. The only *Ovis poli* obtained was one shot by Captain Trotter on a long march of thirty-seven miles. That same day I had my "stalk" of some fine males spoilt by a wolf, which was similarly engaged in approaching them. The horns of the *Ovis poli* and the ibex lie in great numbers (especially the former) at many places on the Pamirs. These animals suffer heavily from the leopards and wolves, which prey almost entirely on them. A murrain is also said to have made great havoc among both some years ago. I brought from the vicinity of the Great Pamir Lake a gigantic pair of *Ovis poli* horns, measuring sixty-five and a half inches in length round the curve, fifty-three inches in a straight line from tip to tip, and sixteen inches round the base. I presented this magnificent head to the British Museum, where it is now to be seen. This large head was exhibited at a meeting of the Zoological Society in London on the 15th of June last by Mr. Edwin Ward, F.Z.S., of Wigmore Street, to whose care I had sent it from India. There was read on that occasion a paper by Sir Victor Brooke on the wild sheep of the Tian Shan and other Asiatic Argali, and reference was made in it to certain points of distinction between the large wild sheep of the Tian Shan and the Pamirs, observed by Captain Biddulph, and also to the statements of the Russian naturalist and traveller, M. Severtzoff, from which it appeared that the Tian Shan species is, in every respect, smaller than that which frequents the Pamirs. The ibex are similar to the Himalayan species, and accordingly differ from those we saw in the Tian Shan range, which were of the black kind, also found in the Kuen Luen. I had the hounds presented by Ali Murdan Shah tried after ibex on the Great Pamir, but though they went eagerly and well after the game, they failed to drive them to the selected rocks, and no opportunity of a shot was given.

We experienced none of the symptoms of great height, viz. headache and difficulty of respiration, on the Pamirs, in the exaggerated degree that native travellers have described. None of our camp followers or people suffered in any unusual way, beyond becoming breathless when exertion was made. All were free from severe headache except our mess butler, who was quite like a mountain barometer in indicating a height of 12,000 feet, as he invariably then became a victim. There was perfect

LARGE OVIS POLI HORNS FROM THE GREAT PAMIR

health among our party throughout the journey. One of the Wakhis who accompanied us with the supplies over the Great Pamir died suddenly from heart disease, on the last march to Aktash, and this was the only casualty or sickness even among the numbers of men who were attached to our camp, when crossing and recrossing the Pamirs. All the natives of India with us worked well and cheerfully through this intensely cold journey, and suffered no bad effects from the severe exposure.

The Pamir plateau may be described as a great, broad, rounded ridge, extending north and south, and crossed by thick mountain chains between which lie elevated valleys, open and gently sloping towards the east, but narrow and confined, with a rapid fall, towards the west. The waters which run in all, with the exception of the eastern flow from the Taghdungbash, collect in the Oxus; the Aksu, from the Little Pamir lake, receiving the eastern drainage which finds an outlet in the Aktash valley, and joining the Murghab, which obtains that from the Alichor and Siriz Pamirs. As the eastern Taghdungbash stream finds its way into the Sirikol and Yarkand rivers, and the Great and Little Karakuls send their waters to the Oxus and the Kashghar river respectively, the Neza Tash range and Kizil Art plain must be regarded as forming the watershed between Eastern and Western Turkistan.

I have explained how the name of a place was mistaken for that of the Little Pamir lake. A similar mistake appears to have been made in the name "Sirikol" given to the lake of Great Pamir. When speaking of and arranging for our journey up to the lake, we were told of halting-places called "Bun, Bekh, and Payan-i-Kul" (base, root, foot of the lake), "Miyan and Barabar-i-Kul" (middle, half-way up the lake), and "Bala and Sir-i-kul" (above and head of the lake). "Sir-i-kul" was most frequently mentioned, being the usual caravan stage, and it was said in such a way as to lead easily to the idea of its being the name of the lake. When the guides were asked pointedly as to the real name of the lake, they answered, "It is called 'Kul-i-Kalan' (the great lake), because there is no other lake here equal to it in size." The name "Kul-i-Sikandar" (Alexander lake), mentioned by a late native traveller, was not recognised by the guides, with whom I used to converse concerning these local details day after day while travelling. Therefore the name "Victoria" given by Wood to the Great Pamir lake displaces no distinctive local one, and may well be introduced into our maps without any risk of causing that geographical confusion, the fear of which made him hesitate to apply it.

Regarding the name "Pamir" the meaning appears to be wilderness, a waste or place abandoned, yet capable of habitation. In answer to my questions as to its application (we were then below the western end of the great lake) one of the guides said, "In former days, when this part was inhabited by Kirghiz, as is shown by the ruins of their villages, the valley was not all called Pamir as it is now. It was then known by its village names, as is the country beyond Sirikol, which being now occupied by Kirghiz, is not known by one name but partly as Charling, Bas Robat, etc. If deserted it would be Pamir." The term appears to be a generic one applied to extensive pasture flats and plains as distinguished from mountain grazing grounds resorted to only in summer. The Shewa plain to the north-east of Faizabad, Badakhshan, celebrated for its summer delights, is also known as the "Shewa Pamir."

We saw a hot sulphurous spring on the bank of the Little Pamir stream at Patur, thirty-five miles below Sarhadd, temperature 130°. Its waters are conducted into several roughly-built stone baths, which are used for rheumatic and other complaints. An equally hot spring in the immediate vicinity disappeared two years ago on the stream-bed extending over it. We also visited the mineral spring near Hissar mentioned by Wood. We found extensive hot springs at Isligh, between the Great Pamir lake and the Aktash valley. The thick grass growing close within their warming influence had been made a resting-place by bears the night before our visit, judging by the quite fresh traces seen all about.

We made repeated inquiries from Kirghiz and Wakhis and from Mir Futteh Ali Shah regarding " Bolor " as a name for any mountain, country, town, river, or place, but all professed perfect ignorance of it. Colonel Yule had previously expressed his opinion with reference to the apocryphal topography of the Oxus regions in which "Bolor" occupied a prominent position, that there was no real evidence for the existence of such a place on the western side of Pamir, and urged its exclusion from geography for the future.

We reached Aktash on the 4th of May, having travelled 157 miles from Kila Panja. Our appointed place of meeting with Captain Biddulph was about three miles beyond the ravine by which the road to Sirikol passes, and allowing for this, we made the Great Pamir route from that place to Kila Panja to be almost exactly the same in distance as that of the Little Pamir, about 185 miles. We were fortunate in finding two days' supplies for our camp awaiting our arrival at Aktash, where they had been sent from Tashkurgan by the Governor according to my request. I had reason to anticipate some difficulty in obtaining a sufficient quantity to subsist the whole party as far as Tashkurgan, and as a provision against failure sent a messenger from Wakhan some days previous to our departure, with a letter to Hussun Shah, asking the assistance which we met at the Aktash frontier as desired. I understood enough of a conversation in the Wakhi dialect that took place in my tent at Langar Kisht between the "Mirzada" and the Aksakal of that village, to make me suspect a deficiency in the amount of food and grain contracted for, and took steps to secure a proper supply; but after the first march I found that through the cupidity and cunning of those entrusted with the Mir's orders to provide, sufficient for five days only instead of eight had been furnished. I at once communicated with the Mir himself on the subject, and received a letter from him the following day, saying how annoyed he was at the dishonesty that had been practised towards us and himself, and promising extra supplies, which reached our camp in good time. We had no fear of being absolutely starved, for seeing horseflesh in common use for food in Kashghar, where, as it is there considered a delicacy, we doubtlessly often ate it in the numerous made dishes at the many feasts we were entertained with, we had learnt to look upon our horses as a last resource always in case of extreme necessity. We halted a day at Aktash to rest our tired animals, and to arrange for the return of the Wakhis to Panja. Fifty of them with fifty-two horses accompanied us on the journey, and rendered us excellent service. We rewarded them liberally, and sent them back with a letter of thanks to their Mir, and a sum of money for the family of "Naoroz," the poor Wakhi who died the previous day. His companions started, carrying the dead body with them for burial at Zong, the deceased's native village.

From Aktash we retraced our steps to Tashkurgan by the same road that we travelled before. The snow had almost entirely disappeared from the Neza Tash pass, and no ice remained in the Shindan defile. But this, which facilitated the journey over the former to the laden horses, increased their difficulties immensely in passage through the latter, as many of the stream crossings which were easy before, over snow and ice, were now hazardous and dangerous, through a wild torrent and over sharp shifting rocks. Some of the baggage animals, weakened by continuous fatiguing work, seemed to succumb under fear, and had to be left in the defile till the following day, to recover from the paralysing numbness which seized upon them. We were again most kindly received and entertained at Tashkurgan by the governor, Hussun Shah.

CAMEL.

DOUBLE-HUMPED CAMEL OF EASTERN TURKISTAN.

CHAPTER XII.

RETURN TOWARDS YARKAND—SUDDEN CHANGE FROM WINTER TO SUMMER—YARKAND—CROPS—SUMMER DRESS OF PEOPLE—LEAVE YARKAND FOR LEH—KOGIAR ROUTE—SNOW-MELTING FLOODS—YANGI-DAWAN PASS—RETURN OF WINTER—KARAKORAM PASS—DEATH OF DR. STOLICZKA—LETTER AND PRESENTS TO MIR FUTTEH ALI SHAH OF WAKHAN—HIS DEATH, AND SUCCESSION OF ALI MURDAN SHAH.

AFTER three days' halt and rest at Tashkurgan we proceeded on our return journey towards Yarkand, accompanied again by our old companion, Hyat Muhammad, the Kirghiz Yuzbashi, whose tents and people we visited on the way some days after. We travelled the first day to the foot of the Kok Moinok pass, taking a long round by the Tagharma plain, where we enjoyed the hospitality of Krumchi Bi, the chief of the Kirghiz located there. We had a long and interesting conversation with him and his Kirghiz about the neighbouring Kizil Art plain and its lakes and streams. This plain, with numerous camels, horses, yaks, sheep, and goats grazing on its fine pasture grounds, was a very pleasant sight to us after the extended wilderness and wastes of the Pamirs. Like the yak, the camel, besides being useful as a beast of burden, also yields raw material for the manufacture of blankets in its long hair and the soft thick undergrowth of down which it gets in winter in common with all animals exposed to the severe cold of these elevated mountain lands. The camel's winter coat is cut in spring, bushy shags being left on the head, neck, humps, and shoulders, as shown in my sketch. Eastern Turkistan is the home of the double-humped camel, whose original stock, in a wild state, is said to be found still in the east, towards Turfan. The domestic species is less in size than the ordinary camel seen in India, and the wild animal is said to be still smaller.

We saw at Tagharma, for the first time, the yak yoked to the plough, but he was led, as he would not be driven, at work. We crossed the Kok Moinok pass (15,800 feet) the following day, and joined the road by which we had travelled up at the little lake on the high Chichiklik plain.

We had a fall of snow at Chihil Gumbaz on the night of the 14th of May, and cold weather till the 18th, when we were at once plunged into extreme heat at Egiz Yar, on the Eastern Turkistan plain. This place was quite "burnt up" with the winter's frosts when we passed through it less than two months before, and now we found it in full summer foliage and verdure. The walnut and apricot trees, which were leafless then, were now bearing fruit as large as marbles, and the crops were up about two feet; vegetation was being rapidly forced by copious irrigation and an atmosphere heated even throughout the night. The water everywhere was thick and brown with a fertilising fine soil, and our drinking supply was obtained by melting lumps of ice, of which every village stores large quantities in deep pits, for the preservation of fruit, and for general use in the hot summer months. From Egiz Yar we struck across country to Kizil Robat, the first stage on the road from Yangi-Hissar to Yarkand.

We reached Yarkand on the 21st May, and halted there a week to rest our tired horses, dispose of those unfit for the severe Karakoram journey still before us, and purchase and hire others to complete our train. The Dadkhwah and his officials were kind and hospitable to the utmost, and we continued to be treated as "honoured guests" to the last, till the frontier at Aktagh (twenty-six miles from the Karakoram pass) was reached.

Yarkand was farther advanced in summer than the Yangi-Hissar neighbourhood; the wheat was higher, and barley was beginning to show in ear, while the fruits were larger, and mulberries were actually ripe. The Lucerne grass was at its full

LADIES' SUMMER FASHIONS, YARKAND.

height, and being cut for cattle and horses. In the dress of the people a great change had also taken place—stout white cotton being worn in place of sheepskin and quilt. For the men the same shaped garments as seen in winter remained, but for the other sex "fashion" produced small, close-fitting, and large dome-like caps and hats of every colour, with flowers stuck coquettishly behind the ears, showing to the front, or fixed to the side of the hat, white robes with scarlet chevrons on the right breast, wide white trousers with scarlet braiding, and embroidered high-heeled shoes with floss-silk rosettes. Coloured gauze wrappers and scarlet garments with white braiding were also worn. The ladies' summer and winter "fashions" of Eastern Turkistan differ most essentially from those of more civilised countries in never changing their style.

We left Yarkand on the 28th May, and the next day reached Kargalik, travelling so far on the same road as that by which we came the previous year. Thence we proceeded by the Kogiar and Yangi-Dawan route to the Yarkand river, up which we passed to Aktagh, where the old road was again joined and followed to Leh, which was reached on the 29th of June 1874. The Kogiar and Yangi-Dawan route avoids the difficult Sanju, and the long Suget passes, but is only practicable for caravans in winter when the upper parts of the Tiznaf and Yarkand streams are in a low and frozen state.

We encountered great difficulties along this road from the melting snow torrents which made the main streams impassable every day for a certain length of time. By the end of a summer's day the sun's heat has reached well into the glacier or snow-bed, and drawn out a stream, which continues running, till in a similar manner the night's cold penetrates to the same depth and shuts up the flowing springs. The duration and extent of the floods and torrents thus produced are affected of course by the state of the day, whether cloudy or bright, and the time of the summer season as regards its degree of heat. Travelling up the streams as we did towards their sources, we met the floods earlier each evening, and were able accordingly to commence our journey sooner each morning. The twisting and turning of the rivers in the narrow valleys and close ravines through which the route passes necessitated innumerable crossings, which in the swollen and turbulent state of the waters became each one more difficult than the other, from the alarm of the horses and mules, and their reluctance to face the tumbling, furious torrent; every crossing was a scene of wild uproar and struggle, and many a load was thrown or dragged under water. The ammunition of the escort was carried in small iron-bound cases, two forming a load, and these being always under the direct care of a guard were generally supposed to contain treasure. One of the ponies so loaded was swept down the stream into a deep pool, where in getting it ashore one of the boxes slipped and was lost in the depths. The Yarkandis seemed to take particular notice of the spot, and doubtlessly the place was disappointedly visited with the object of recovering the lost treasure when the stream fell low enough to admit of search for it.

A heavy fall of snow on the night of the 8th of June enabled us to cross the Yangi-Dawan pass (16,000 feet), and traverse the deep rocky gorge leading from it down to the Yarkand river, with comparative ease. The gorge was filled with masses of ice, broken up by the action of the summer torrents; and the head-quarter party of the Mission, which preceded us, had made this passage with much difficulty and labour. The greater cold and the gloom following upon the previous night's snowfall kept the stream down, and we worked our way over the ice blocks and fissures without the fear of troubling torrents as usual. We were fortunate in this respect with falls of snow on the 11th, 12th, 13th, and 16th June, as we pursued our journey over the Karakoram towards Leh. The return of cold weather checked the flow of the streams long enough to allow us to pass easily, and we met with no difficulties from floods in that part of the road as experienced by Mr. Forsyth's party which had passed before us.

Three days after crossing the Karakoram pass, while journeying by the elevated Dipsang route mentioned at page 21, we suffered the deep affliction of losing by death one of our party, Dr. Stoliczka, a highly valued friend and talented companion. This sad event has deprived the scientific world of much of the great store of knowledge which Dr. Stoliczka laid up in Tibet and Turkistan; for although his notes and papers on the special subjects of his research were preserved, and the result of his labours is to be given to it under most competent guidance, still it is not to be expected that the work can be produced in the perfect form that it would have assumed had the gifted author been spared to complete it. He was buried at Leh, where a handsome memorial tablet has been erected over his tomb by the Government of India.

Mir Futteh Ali Shah of Wakhan died in the early part of this year, and was succeeded by his son, Ali Murdan Shah. It was a matter of great satisfaction to us that the old Mir, who, as I mentioned, was feeble and infirm from age, lived long enough to receive the letter and valuable presents which the Viceroy of India caused to be sent to him on our return, in acknowledgment of his kind hospitality, aid, and protection to us. The letter and presents were safely delivered by a trusty native officer, who proceeded with them from Peshawur; and replies were received from both father and son, expressing great pleasure at being remembered by their English friends.

www.ingramcontent.com/pod-product-compliance
Lightning Source LLC
Chambersburg PA
CBHW032113230426
43672CB00009B/1721